PRACTICING EFFECTIVE MANAGEMENT

PRACTICING EFFECTIVE MANAGEMENT

ELTON T. REEVES

amacom

A DIVISION OF AMERICAN MANAGEMENT ASSOCIATIONS

Library of Congress Cataloging in Publication Data

Reeves, Elton T
    Practicing effective management.

    1. Management. I. Title.
HD38.R36   658.4   75-4906
ISBN 0-8144-5398-8

First Printing

To four wonderful grandchildren
Jennie, Kirk, Katie, and Amy Liz

CONTENTS

	Introduction	1
1	Group Managerial Philosophy	13
2	Individual Managerial Philosophy	25
3	The Responsibilities of a Manager	36
4	The Manager and Innovation	44
5	The Manager as a Censor	58
6	The Manager as a Parent Figure	69
7	The Manager and Social Responsibility	83
8	The Manager and Developmental Activities	95
9	Peer Relationships of the Manager	109
10	Duties to the Enterprise vs. Duties to Self	120
11	The Managerial Mentality	131
12	So Now Where?	142

A NOTE TO THE READER

This book is addressed to all managers of both sexes. Unfortunately, wordcrafters in English have so far not come up with a generally acceptable term to include both male and female members of management. It is hoped that readers will accept the "he's" and "his's" in these pages as being referent to both sexes.

ELTON T. REEVES

INTRODUCTION

There are some managers who would argue that, first, it is probably impossible to state a philosophy of management and, second, even if it were possible there is no need to have it propounded. The number of managers of this kind is greater than we like to think, and each contributes his or her little bit to the general air of chaos and confusion which typifies some managerial areas. Under the belief that the determination and statement of a philosophy of management should be a help to any member of that group, our first question is then one of enablement.

TRAITS OF A MANAGEMENT PHILOSOPHER

To develop a philosophy in any area, the philosopher must have a certain amount of time for reflection and synthesis. In other words, those who are intensely concerned with the minutiae of daily living will never produce a philosophy. This contemplative, introspective attitude is not a natural one for most people; careful cultivation and practice are needed to achieve this sort of mental set.

Another attribute which the philosopher must develop to a fine degree is the ability to be coldly analytical of observed behavior and its causes. If he is to advance from the specific to the general in his thinking, the philosopher must be quite certain of what is going on about him and why it is happening. This is the point at which he, as observer, must separate himself entirely from any personal feelings he may have about the people being observed. It is a difficult task, but a necessary one, that the philosopher assess the behavior of his friends and enemies as well as of those whom he scarcely knows and do it in such a manner that his observations are not skewed by his personal emotions.

A third requirement for the would-be philosopher is that he have the ability to see relationships between events in the light of causes and effects. Not everyone can do this; in fact, a huge majority of human beings live all their lives with no perception of a cause-and-effect relationship in the events of their environment. The emerging philosopher will actually come into being only if he can do this regularly in his surroundings.

The philosopher in any field, but especially in management, must be particularly articulate in his communications with his fellows. What he will be communicating in most cases will be strange to his listeners; it is essential that these communications be clear and lucid for understanding to result among all concerned.

Next, the philosopher must be totally unafraid to face the new, strange, and even threatening things he meets in his working world. It is these new things which will structure the changes in an emerging philosophy of management. In this particular facet of his personality the philosopher will show his greatest variance from the norm. Most of us still have a few butterflies when we are first exposed to new things. The philosopher too experiences an excitation of his adrenal glands, but it manifests itself in anticipatory excitement rather than in fear. He likes change.

Another requisite for the philosopher, often overlooked by those aspiring to be creative in any field, is historical awareness. Creation of the new can never happen "on purpose" unless the person concerned has a deep and intimate knowledge of the old things in his discipline. Creative ideation depends on the ability to compare and judge the proposed new items against already established norms. The only reason for producing something new *should* be to improve on what has gone before. We are deluged with a sea of new things that have no real reason for being, since they are an improvement on nothing. We shall have more to say about this later.

Finally, the philosopher must be especially well endowed in conceptual skills. This highly desirable kind of intelligence is not as widespread as some other types. The ability to envision the new thing quickly is a must for the philosopher to be. Filling in details can be left to others, but the general shape and scope of the new creation has to come from the philosopher himself. This is a reiteration of what we have said before: The philosopher must not be afraid to be a pioneer and must be comfortable in being the first person in a new territory. In fact, for a large part of his existence, he must not even care whether he is being followed by anyone else!

None of this is to imply that the philosopher is a loner. He will be constantly drawing upon the thoughts and actions of his fellow workers, his line of management, and his peers. They will be giving him the raw materials for his own construction, and their continuity of this process is mandatory for his success. This ability to live with others, communicate with them, take what they offer and adapt it to his own needs, and still maintain good relationships with them is the characteristic which sets the philosopher apart from his fellows. He is an impersonal observer, but he makes very personal use of his observations for his own good and that of his associates.

In these few words we have perhaps answered the question of whether there can be a philosophy of management. The answer is an unqualified yes. We have also seen that those who produce these philosophies are special people. They need special handling, special training, and special understanding by those with whom they work, because their labors will have direct impact on everyone in the working group, both immediately and in the future. We are living in a time of unbelievably swift change in every aspect of our world, and the management field is no exception. The questions to be answered are: Is a change needed here? If so, does the proposed change satisfy our needs? Is it the *right* change to propose and implement?

Because of his special qualities, the philosopher should be

given special consideration as he answers these questions for us. His perceptions are probably better than ours, and we should defer to his judgment in most cases if it varies from our own. It follows that the philosopher cannot afford to be wrong as many times as the average manager and still hold his position of leadership among his peers. If our philosophy is wrong, our entire fabric of living is based on a false foundation, and nothing but trouble can come from that.

All right, then, if we are agreed that it is possible to achieve a philosophy of management, how do we get there from here? The rest of this volume will be spent in answering that question.

WHO DETERMINES THE MANAGERIAL PHILOSOPHY?

We have thus far spoken in the abstract of the managerial need to establish a philosophy of management for every enterprise. But who will actually do this for each organization? In the ideal situation, the leader of the group formulates and communicates the philosophy before the group actually sets down its first objectives and goals. Unfortunately, this is often not the way it is done. In too many cases, businesses are begun almost whimsically — apparently on an impulse by the originators. People see the possibility for making a quick buck, so they jump into the business of snaring the loose dollar and they are off. This kind of action is almost always doomed to failure, either immediately or in a short while. What we are saying is that every ongoing enterprise must have a rationale, and it must be run within the dictates of that rationale to be successful.

If the owner/leader of the organization does not formulate and communicate his philosophy of doing business, someone in the group will do it for him. This is never too satisfactory. Most working people demand a reason for doing what they do at work. If none is given to them by their bosses, they will invent one for themselves. Human dignity demands that we not be blind slaves, that we have a logical reason for performing our tasks at whatever level we are laboring. A managerial philosophy which is formulated by subordinates rather than leaders simply to fill a void is not likely to be a neat or very helpful instrument. Nor is it likely to do the job for which it is intended. There will of necessity be too many gaps in the structure, and this will lead to continuing frustration on the part of the working members of the group.

The most viable and desirable method of structuring the philosophy of a work group is for the leaders to sketch the broad limits and then delegate to lower echelons the authority and responsibility for filling in the details, subject to monitoring by the group's top management at any time. This is the basic requirement for any sort of participative management, which is the methodology best suited to job satisfaction for most employees. But the leaders must constantly be aware that this cannot be done satisfactorily unless the people in the organization have been trained to accept and operate under this responsibility. We can never simply say to them: "Go do this philosophizing." This is too threatening. They must be made ready for this new activity by education, training, and practice. It is a variation of the old saw that we walk before we run.

One of the things every manager must keep in mind continually is that a philosophy cannot be built in a vacuum. As the employee starts to flesh out his concept of doing business, it is incumbent upon him to communicate at every step of the way with both his manager and his peers; and, of the two, perhaps the latter is the more important. The boss can correct what he perceives as errors in a subordinate's thinking at any time; peers don't have this authority over their fellows, but two-way communication will have a beneficial effect on the thinking of the entire group, and fatal flaws will be identified as they surface in the communicative process.

There is nothing wrong with using an empirical method in building a philosophy of management, if we are doing it for ourselves alone. Trial and error is a way of life for most of us. The important thing is to be able to discern and rectify our errors quickly, before they have done irreparable damage to our operation. In fact, psychologically, the learning we do from our mistakes is probably the best form of learning.

However, it is another thing to attempt to build a philosophy of management for others — that is, an "official" philosophy for the entire enterprise. In this case we need at least reasonable assurance that the product we impose on others is free from major flaws. This means that at some point in time not too remote each facet of the philosophy will have to be tried and tested before it is adopted by the group. It is for this reason that experience remains the best asset for any person entering management, and this fundamental verity will always be with us. This is not to say that managers must be graybeards; they must, if youthful, be able to make valid judgments of what is done by others and then be willing to be guided by these judgments in their own actions.

For the greatest possible commitment of all members of the group, the development of a managerial philosophy should be a team effort. The word "team" implies two things: cooperation from everyone and the utilization of special skills and abilities of each member of the group. The analogy to the modern football team is inescapable. A professional football team is composed of a number of players who perform esoteric specialties, each designed and developed to make a specific contribution to the actions of the entire team. The same should be true in a managerial team.

Business and industry today are so complex and involuted that only the very top leaders can afford the luxury of being generalists. All other layers of management must work most of the time in their area of specialty, and the contributions of each manager will be measured in the discipline in which he or she has been trained. This is as it should be. By the same token, if top management has provided proper guidance and leadership, each manager will be able to make a specific contribution to the overall philosophy of the enterprise.

It is obvious that the best answer to the question of who is to determine the philosophy of management is: "Everyone with any managerial responsibility in the group." It is equally obvious that this is not the case — yet — in the real world. In many, perhaps even a majority of, businesses the philosophy of management is imposed by fiat from above. Many of these businesses continue to be successful, even with this handicap. But a true handicap it is, and it is interesting to speculate how much *more* successful these enterprises would be if all members of management were given a share of the responsibility and its concomitant authority. This single thing can furnish much of the nourishment needed for managerial growth and development in any business or industry.

HOW IS A MANAGERIAL PHILOSOPHY COMMUNICATED?

The best managerial philosophy in the world cannot work unless it is communicated thoroughly and understood by all affected. There are some special constraints about its communication which must be observed by all managers. These should be completely understood and agreed to by everyone before startup time.

Item: Complete and official communication of a philosophy of management must be withheld until its adoption by top management is certain. If all thinking in this area is completely disseminated, a great deal of confusion will result, since there will inevitably be many changes in thinking before the final result is set in concrete. The troops not only will be confused but will probably begin to lose faith in their leadership, since they think they are seeing a lack of decisiveness at the top. The leaders themselves will not have this feeling about their actions, since, as we have seen, the formulation of a managerial philosophy is often a trial-and-error process. But employees need to have an unshakable faith and trust in the actions and decisions of top management in order to maintain their mental health and to be able to do a good job from day to day.

Item: The corollary of this principle is just as important. As soon as part or all of a managerial philosophy for a firm is adopted, it should be communicated immediately to all employees. If it is to be the navigational instrument it should be for all workers, they need to have it the moment it is operational, so as to become acquainted with it and make themselves comfortable working within it.

Item: The managements of many firms are unwilling to commit their philosophies to writing. There are many reasons for this. The most common one is uneasiness from the possibility that there will later be a major shift in philosophy; if this occurs, the presence of a written document which is becoming outmoded is an embarrassment to management. This should not be the case, but if it is, management is probably correct in not writing it out and circulating it. This means that it is more important than ever to disseminate the philosophy orally to everyone. Here the question becomes one of assuring that the listeners have a real understanding of what is being communicated. The manager can never be certain of this simply by asking if the listener understands. Naturally, the answer will be yes, even though the person being asked may be completely in the dark.

We all have our pride, and we hate to admit that we don't understand what someone else is saying to us. Therefore, the manager who is giving an oral outline of the philosophy to an employee should insist on feedback of such a kind that it can be positively determined whether the employee understands what is being said. The way to get this feedback is to ask the listener to paraphrase what he has heard. If he can do this satisfactorily, it is almost certain that the necessary understanding is there.

Item: A managerial philosophy should be communicated in the context of its usage. That is, management should give frequent examples of how the philosophy is expected to affect the behavior of the employees on the job. The purpose of a philosophy is just that: to act as a control on the actions and work habits of the employees of the enterprise. Unless that happens, the objectives of the philosophy are vitiated, and the exercise has been sterile and useless. We shall discuss this matter more later on.

Item: The manager should not fall into the trap of assuming that a one-shot communication will accomplish the entire job. The more important the message, the more certain we can be that not one, or two, but many communicative efforts must be made to get the message across. Just think of how many times we have to reiterate certain maxims and fundamental truths to children before we can be sure they really understand them and are ready to be guided by them in their daily living. The same situation holds for adults in the work scene. The manager must stand ready to repeat his message as many times as necessary to assure its reception and acceptance. If there is the slightest doubt that it has been well received, the manager must be ready to do it again.

Item: It is probable that advantage will be found in communicating a firm's philosophy to many people outside the group of employees. Customers have a vested interest in knowing how an enterprise is run before they buy its products. Vendors too need to know how a firm's management thinks and does business so that they can best serve it as customers.

Item: The one imperative above all is that the communication of the finished philosophy be honest and complete. The general public is rapidly becoming so sophisticated that any ongoing degree of hypocrisy will quickly be discovered and exposed. The day is passing when we can say one thing and do another in our business dealings. As of about the day after tomorrow we shall be forced to declare our true positions and then be prepared to live by them with everyone with whom we have any dealings. The entire base must be covered truthfully as well. We cannot afford to leave out an important segment of the explanation of how we do business and then act in accordance with an unpublished agenda. The public is no longer in a mood to stand still for that, either. It's a real case of "the truth, the whole truth, and nothing but the truth."

Item: Any obvious ancillary effects expected from our way of doing business should be communicated to all parties. There may be some ripples from the rock we throw into the pond, and the public has a right to know this if we expect certain things to happen as a result of our doing business. If these results do not materialize no harm is done, but at least we have been honest in dealing with the public and will get recognition for that honesty.

This communicative aspect of the managerial duty of philosophizing will be time-consuming to a moderate degree, but the results will more than pay for the time involved.

BEHAVIORAL EFFECTS OF A MANAGER'S PHILOSOPHY

We can be certain that the gradual evolution of a philosophy, or the quick adoption of a ready-made one, will have noticeable effects on the behavior of the managers involved. This is because a philosophy has as its reason for being the guidance of actions of those subscribing to it. For example, at its highest and best level, a philosophy is a moral code that determines the actions of its subscribers, designating certain behavior as "good" or "bad." Many people are not so much immoral as amoral; they have no consciences and are therefore not circumscribed in their interactions with others or worried about the possible outcomes of those actions. We could make a good case for the proposal that the greatest good which can come from the adoption of the right kind of philosophy is the restraint it puts on dysfunctional actions on the part of a manager.

By the same token, we cannot fail to recognize that if the managerial philosophy adopted by individuals or groups is "bad," we may expect their actions to have undesirable effects on those with whom they interface. According to their lights, and under the philosophy by which they operate, the Mafia are not doing wrong, but are simply looking out for themselves and the "family." This to them is the highest good; others have no individual rights if they come into conflict with the family.

A carefully designed and workable managerial philosophy will be the best possible agent of change for managerial behavior. Once it is understood that a philosophy demands a particular kind of behavior, and once the philosophy has been truly adopted by the managerial group, any necessary change in behavior will follow automatically, even if it means changing habits which have been years in the making. The reason, of course, is the high level of motivation which will be present for making the change, and this is the first requisite for extinguishing one habit and substituting another for it.

A good managerial philosophy will often cause the managers operating under it to see for themselves desirable or necessary behavioral changes and will spur them to initiate these changes voluntarily. We could even go so far as to say that an effective philosophy will act as both a power plant and a navigational instrument for the career of the managers involved. It is essential that something perform this function; nothing else will do it quite so well as a finely articulated and comprehensive managerial philosophy which is kept up to date and in step with the changing times.

The manager who adopts a philosophy and follows it closely will soon learn that it can help him gather a data bank for his behavior. Templates are established for the prejudgment of proposed actions, and results of actions already taken can be quickly evaluated as well. Essentially, what we are saying here is that a good philosophy of management will have the effect of making the manager a reasoning and reasonable human being in the discharge of his duties. If we are properly equipped philosophically, we can forecast desirable behavior for almost any situation in which we find ourselves, and this is an advantage seldom equaled in our other business activities. It is mandatory that we do this in order to be successful, but it is hard to find another method of accomplishing this necessary objective.

Thus far, we have been considering only that behavior initiated by the manager on his own. We should also be aware that a managerial philosophy will help in determining our *reactive* behavior—that is, what we do when another person interfaces with us and begins some action. To be consistent, our behavior in these situations must be entirely consonant with our philosophy; we can never afford to deviate from the guidelines imposed by our fundamental beliefs. Thus our philosophy will serve to modulate our maturity as individuals and will definitely help keep us on the right road.

This is especially true when we are faced with hostility from others. A good philosophy will have foreseen this eventuality, as well as nearly all other kinds of circumstances, and will have indicated the proper behavior for it. We can save ourselves many embarrassments, or seriously bad results, if our managerial philosophy takes over as an automatic pilot when we are threatened by others. When we have preprogrammed our reactions, we will be much less likely to panic and commit mistakes which will come back to haunt us later.

With a good philosophy of management for a backup, we will be much more creative in our behavior. We will be alert for situations which will force us to innovate in order to get where we want to go, and we will be continuously evaluating our proposed innovations for their results if implemented. As noted before, innovation for its own sake is quite likely to result only in wasted effort and lost resources. There has to be a reason for it before we make the sacrifices attendant upon designing and launching new things. Therefore, it is incumbent upon us to know when it is desirable or necessary to create something new and when it is better to go along with an existing and proven tool to get desired results.

Just a moment ago we examined our reactive interpersonal relations. It is necessary to recognize that a good managerial philosophy will also have a beneficial effect on relationships which we initiate ourselves. There will be fewer thoughtless actions resulting in abrasions in our interpersonal relationships, with perhaps some irremediable ruptures. Any of these which we can avert is clearly pure gain in our human ledgers.

The important thing to remember is that an operant managerial philosophy will actively help the manager by giving him direction, steadiness, and prejudgment of his behavior on the job, with concomitant advantages which will be invaluable in helping him develop into a mature manager.

1

GROUP
MANAGERIAL
PHILOSOPHY

Managerial philosophy is dichotomized. In order to get the entire perspective, we must consider both the managerial philosophy of the work group as a whole and the individual philosophies of the members of the group. It must be remarked here that there cannot be too much divergence between them, or the resulting situation will be intolerable; at the same time, there will always be some small differences between them. This is as it should be, if we are to have proper regard for the individualism of the various managers involved. We shall consider the matter of the group philosophy first, then look at individuals.

EVOLUTION OF A GROUP PHILOSOPHY

We have already said that the ideal situation for the group is to have the top leadership outline the general parameters of the philosophy of the group and then delegate the filling in of details to the rest of management. Hopefully, this is what the individual manager will find in his work environment and in the entire enterprise. When this happens, the givens of management are properly considered, and individual managers can work more comfortably in helping to build a philosophy.

The one point we must keep constantly in mind is that no philosophy can be static. It must evolve as dictated by the total environment, or the philosophy and the enterprise will both succumb. The point of division, and the area where managers must make their decisions concerning their philosophies, is when the enterprise will allow the environment to shape its philosophy and when it will be more prudent to act unilaterally and force the environment to accede to the needs of the business. This can sometimes be done, but the perception of these times and their desirability must be the product of the judgmental thinking of the managers concerned. These are make-or-break decisions and are not to be entered into lightly by any manager or any enterprise.

It should be immediately apparent that the managerial philosophy of any group will in all probability start out rather simple and uncomplicated. All of us have a tendency to make assumptions about the essential simplicity of our guidance systems and to learn later, by hard experience, that such uncomplicated guidelines do not cover all fronts. Two factors are involved here: Both our civilization and our enterprise are becoming more complex day by day, and what started out as a pretty simple, bare-bones Ten Commandments eventually will wind up as a rather wordy and involved Torah. We need more than just a broadly sketched map by which to chart our business courses.

However, great care must be exerted by all managers to make sure that their group philosophy does not grow simply by expediency. We have to be smart enough to foresee trends, anticipate changes, and be ready for them before they are upon us, forcing us into hasty and ill-considered actions which may boomerang. Of this, more later.

What we have, then, is the possibility of two different situations arising. The first, as we have seen, is when our environment changes and forces us to modify our philosophy in order to stay in step at all. This means the manager must be especially alert to and aware of changes as they are just beginning, in order to alter his thinking and make plans for the necessary adjustments. These, like any other changes to be implemented within the organization, will take a lot of planning, a lot of coordination, and a lot of work on the part of all concerned. Leadtimes of months are often necessary to get something new into the philosophical aspects of our work, let alone to translate it into day-to-day action on the floor. The sooner we get started on these things, the better chance we will have that they will suffice.

The second situation arises when the manager sees a change needed in managerial philosophy which is not necessarily dictated by the outside situation. In other words, this is something which he will originate by himself, or which the group will undertake unilaterally, and will then prepare for implementation in the same manner as mentioned before. In either event, about the same leadtimes and preparatory actions will be entailed, as well as voluminous and specific communication to all hands to make certain that everyone understands.

The title of this segment of the chapter contains the word "evolution." This is exactly descriptive of the process by which a group managerial philosophy should come about. Stresses and vectors, acting both internally and externally upon management, will bring about reactions in the guidance mechanism by which the business is run.

We must also take into account the synergy which a healthy and properly functioning group of managers will display. This means that the performance of the group as a whole will be greater than the individual contributions of the members. This is one of the inherent benefits of working groups, because groups can do more than the total efforts of the members. Were it not for this self-evident fact, there would be nothing gained from forming working groups, and we could all remain in the personally more comfortable situation of being individual contributors, with no responsibility toward the other employees of our company or agency. This, of course, is an insupportable situation, since it approaches anarchy and denigrates every principle on which our nation was founded.

WHO CONTRIBUTES AND WHEN?

We have already noted two ways by which a group managerial philosophy may be evolved: It can be laid down by top management (which is really the surer way that all will be satisfied), or, failing that, the members of management can do it by themselves, with attendant possibility of some misunderstandings and failure to satisfy all objectives of the enterprise. But a third and much more satisfying way is to have top management give the broad outlines and then have the rest of the management team fill in the details area by area.

It is meaningful when each specialty and each discipline contributes that part germane to its activities. Engineers should contribute the philosophical basics for the engineering function; fiscal people should supply the money elements; industrial relations specialists should have inputs for the people side of the philosophy. None of this is to say that any of these experts should not be challenged if their contributions are less than satisfactory to others. In the final analysis, *all* managers must be fairly well satisfied with the company philosophy if it is to work at all.

It must be remembered that no manager is ready to make a contribution toward the group philosophy until he has thought it through in his most mature manner. This is no place for "off the top of the head," impulsive contributions; the entire group of managers will be examining every facet of the final product, and no one wants to be embarrassed by putting in shallow planks.

In this kind of group-think activity, there must be a coordinator. Top management should clearly designate the person or persons responsible for receiving the inputs of the rest of management, and the other managers should adhere to this absolutely. When this is done, the coordinator will be able to act as a preliminary screening device, examining contributions as they come in, since he will be familiar with the rest of the growing philosophy. Better to process these thoughts carefully now than to adopt them loosely, in haste, and have them rise up and haunt management later.

The matter of when the contributions are to be made is a little more uncertain than the question of who will make offerings. One consideration to keep in mind is that for each area of major decision making a philosophy should be operational before the decisions are made. We cannot hope to do a good job in guiding our corporate ship unless we have adequate navigational instruments, and that is what a company philosophy really is. When there are guidelines, it is much easier for managers to make meaningful decisions about the job.

A second thing to be aware of is that we should be prepared to examine and judge new ideas *when they are presented.* Nothing can be more stultifying to managerial creativity than to have its products ignored when they are offered. If a manager, or a group of managers, comes up with some fresh thinking about the company's philosophy, it should be given an immediate, objective, and impartial hearing. The time to do this is when it appears, not some weeks or months later.

By the same token, the alert and conscientious manager will be thinking constantly in this area and will make every effort to forestall needs for philosophizing before they arise. It is best to be prepared beforehand for the times when it will be mandatory to refer to an operational philosophy in making decisions. We could say then, quite correctly, that a good management team will work hard to synthesize a philosophy and have it in shape when the time comes to apply it to everyday working affairs.

Even so, it is nearly inevitable that any modern business on any given day will find itself faced with a situation for which there is no philosophical plank available. This is where management will have to patch around its short circuit and then come back later to make a permanent new installation for this need. The important and very necessary thing to do here is to make certain that all hands know this is an emergency procedure, and that later reconsideration of what has happened may result in changing the emergency guidelines laid down for this one case.

A thinking manager will also recognize that it will occasionally be necessary for him to *force* a "right time" for the introduction of a new philosophy. Analysis of the situation may show that right here and now the company is facing a new combination of circumstances which will put a different light on everything. It then behooves the manager to prepare his people for the introduction of a new philosophy and policy designed to meet this specific set of circumstances. Developing this sort of expertise is a defensive weapon of inestimable value for the manager. It can forestall many uncomfortable or even dangerous moments and will be fine insurance for the success of the manager.

This same sort of "preventive maintenance" in the philosophical field can be entered into profitably by a group of managers in an enterprise, or perhaps by the entire managerial population. The occurrence of unforeseen happenings is not limited to only a part of the company; the whole may be faced with something for which no provision has been made. However, the process is the same whether only one manager or the entire membership of management is involved. In the latter case, of course, group cooperation and coordination will be necessary so that effective action can be taken and proper communication made. Only then will the entire work force know what is going on and be prepared for it.

Herein lies one of the graver faults of management throughout our country. There are numberless cases where a failure on management's part to forewarn all employees of the possibility of some event happening has resulted in grave injury to the entire enterprise or its demise. When we ask who contributes and when to the formulation of a group philosophy of management, the "right" answer is: "Everyone, whenever the need arises, or preferably before the need is felt."

FLEXIBILITY OR INFLEXIBILITY?

The question of how flexible a company philosophy should be requires some of the more delicate decisions on the part of management as the daily scene unfolds. The first consideration is that the philosophy *not* be wishy-washy. It must not be so lightly anchored that the first little puff of wind from the opposition can topple it. If it has been properly conceptualized, and if the mature thinking of all of management has been exercised in considering the parts, it should be able to stand up to a considerable onslaught by those opposed to its principles.

This resistance to whimsical attack on the company's basic philosophy must be ingrained into managerial thinking, until it is nearly a conditioned reflex. For self-serving reasons, many people both inside and outside the organization will try to destroy the guidelines by which a firm is run. It is against these natural enemies that management must present a strong, united front and be ready to go into battle whenever necessary.

The ideal arrangement is to have several built-in shock absorbers to take up the initial force of any attack. An example is the company which has established a standing committee, usually of middle managers and executives, to consider all matters pertaining to possible changes in policy or philosophy. The members of this group must never surrender to panic in their deliberations but must be sure that they have the necessary data to make a reasoned response and to come up with the correct decision for each situation brought before them. In fact, in large and complex organizations, these committee members might well devote full time to all problems arising in the areas of policy or company philosophy, and if they function properly they will more than pay their way by the good they accomplish for the enterprise.

The trick, of course, is in making proper selection of the member of such a committee. It must be noted that no position as such should carry automatic membership in the committee. The choice should always be made after very careful evaluation of each person being considered for appointment. Once made, the decision must be defended vigorously against any attack by those who have an ax to grind.

Another point worth noting is that there must be absolutely no secrets held from the committee. Its members must have full access to any and all company data, whether open or closely guarded proprietary matters. If they can be trusted enough to be appointed to this crucial committee, they must be trusted the rest of the way and given without question whatever information they need to do their job. This is one of the hardest things for top managements to do, because they value so highly the store of "privileged information" they carry.

There is an additional advantage inherent in this arrangement that is not often perceived by executive echelons: By acting in this way, they are giving invaluable training to potential candidates for the executive level of management and will be preparing replacements for those executives about to retire.

This is a matter too often overlooked, to the ultimate harm of the company. In fact, it would be a very interesting (but hard-to-come-by) statistic to discover how many firms have gone under because they have failed to prepare replacements for their key executive positions. Especially vulnerable to such a fate is the enterprise formed by a group of young men and women of about the same age, at a time in their lives when none of them thinks of aging and retirement. This group may then grow old together, to be faced at some later stage with the calamitous knowledge that *all* of them will be disappearing from the scene at nearly the same time and that proper replacements have not been prepared for any of them.

We would be at fault if we failed to look at the other side of this coin. We might get the erroneous idea that rigidity is the password for the day—and it most certainly is not. There are many reasons which might make us properly alter the guidelines by which we run a business. The first, and most common, is when outside factors have changed grossly, and in these times that can happen twice a day and three times on Friday.

What must be remembered is that every change in the outside mix must be evaluated separately and a considered decision made each time. This should be a cooperative effort of all management personnel, as stated before. No one person should ever have total responsibility for making such a decision, except perhaps in a closely held entrepreneurship, and even there the owner would do well to listen to others before committing himself to a radical change. At the same time, he should not be deaf to the signals he receives about the changes which are occurring around him.

A second situation that may require reassessment of company guidelines is when changes occur internally. Every time new product lines are considered, an intensive look should be made to see how these will affect the company philosophy. Any sort of diversification, with its attendant increase in complexity of the organization, will require attention from the monitors of the policy. This activity just might result in a decision to abandon the proposed new products, if their effect on the company would be too severe.

Personnel movements, such as new hires, promotions, replacements, and reorganizations, will also require attention. Once again, flexibility will be necessary in adjusting to these new arrangements. A change in the occupant of an important box in the organizational chart will almost invariably require some modification of the guidelines, since no two people ever exhibit identical behavior patterns in the same job. In fact, the job is *not* the same when a new incumbent appears. Every person modifies his job according to his personality and methods of operation; this will probably require some change in the company philosophy to keep it viable.   ˙

To recapitulate, we have to be constantly alert to the situation about us to determine whether we will hold the line and not modify the philosophy or whether it would be more effective and advantageous to make some changes in it. The degree of flexibility or inflexibility must at all times be a careful management decision, taken only after mature consideration and examination of all available data.

WHAT DOES A GROUP PHILOSOPHY CONTROL?

We have gone to some trouble to determine how a group goes about conceptualizing its philosophy. Now the question is, after it is formulated, what aspects of the group's activities does the philosophy control, or at least monitor? There are several. First, the philosophy will shape the methodology of interaction among the members of the group. Mannerisms, approaches, norms of behavior, all will come under the influence of the master template as exemplified by the philosophy. Group members will feel at ease when they are conforming to preestablished guidelines in their daily interfaces;

conversely, they will be extremely ill at ease unless they are within the established patterns of behavior. This is no different at work, of course, than it is in other areas of life, but it is of particular importance at the work station, since so much of our effectiveness is determined by the ease of interaction.

One of the fallouts from this situation is that the philosophy of the group will directly state the protocol. One philosophy will demand a rigid, castelike type of structure; another will dictate an extremely informal relationship among the various levels of management in which status symbols are nearly nonexistent. Most philosophies will fall somewhere within these two extremes. Once again, it should be noted that the great majority of us are more comfortable operating somewhere in the middle, rather than being the cynosure of all eyes because we 'are at one end or the other of a spectrum of this kind.

A second vector controlled by the group's philosophy is the actual collection of working methods. Under one philosophy, it might be possible to use a particular method without any question; under another philosophy, this method might be completely forbidden and never considered for use. Managers who are sensitive to their surroundings will not have too much trouble determining at once whether a proposed method is consonant with the group's philosophy or antithetical to it. Once this determination has been made, the rest is easy. It will be "go" or "no go" according to this criterion.

This is perhaps the most cogent argument for the formulation and adoption of a group philosophy. Until a philosophy is developed, the group will be struggling in a search for methodology and will be continually confused because of a lack of clarity as to how to proceed. The same laws of group dynamics apply here as in any other group situation: Cohesiveness will be increased by taking action according to the dictates of a common philosophy; sanctions will be quickly applied to anyone in the group who deviates from the established norms; a persistent deviant will become an isolate after a short time and will totally lose his effectiveness in the group. We must remember these facts continually as we guide our individual courses through the managerial life; failure to do so can be tragic.

A third vector controlled by the group philosophy is the way we approach others outside the group. Our business associations with these people will tend to become fairly formalized, but this formality will follow special guidelines made completely logical by our overriding philosophy. Again, this becomes a method for making our life easier and less complicated, since we will not have to search frantically for an approach every time we have contact with strangers from outside our group. Because we know how we are going to approach them, we can also predict with reasonable certainty how they will react to us, and this makes for an easier introduction and quicker achievement of a smooth working relationship.

This does not mean that there is anything automatic or ritualistic about our interactions with others. There will always be atypical cases because of individual differences among people; but for the most part we can be fairly certain that our readings will be accurate and that we can come more quickly to a viable working relationship with others. The importance of this is hard to exaggerate for the busy manager on today's scene.

Another vector controlled by the group philosophy is the manner in which we approach those below us in the business hierarchy, whether they are other managers or nonmanagerial personnel. This is important, because they will have their own expectations as to how managers should react with them, and failure to meet these expectations will be quite upsetting to them. This matter is more important than many managers realize. The contract an employee makes with his management is one of the most important he will ever make, since it controls the major part of his waking life.

Again, this is one of the reasons it is of such overwhelming importance that the philosophy be communicated thoroughly and clearly to *all* employees. They have no way of reconciling your behavior with their expectations unless they know the guidelines under which you are operating. It would be interesting to know how much business and industrial turnover is caused by this one factor alone. People simply will not remain where they can find no meeting of the minds with their supervision and management. They will take off for more comfortable surroundings, and the money the company has invested in them will have been a needless waste.

In this chapter we have made an effort to describe the method by which a group of managers develops its philosophy and to indicate some of the factors which this philosophy will control once it is propounded. It is important that all managers remember constantly how this action will give guidance to their behavior. Without it, they will be adrift without a compass on a pretty rough sea.

2

INDIVIDUAL MANAGERIAL PHILOSOPHY

If it is true that a group of managers must have a common philosophy by which to run their enterprise, then it is even more certain that individuals must have a personal philosophy by which to guide their lives. Unless a person does, he or she is forever veering on and off course, and a lifetime spent like this can only be less than satisfactory. The question, then, is: How do we get there from here?

DEVELOPING A PHILOSOPHY IS A MATURATION PROCESS

No immature person ever has a personal philosophy, unless we were to suppose that *not* having one could be called a philosophy. People can be truly said to be mature intellectually and emotionally when they have evolved a philosophy which is satisfactory and workable for them. The one point of which we must remind ourselves constantly is that maturing is not a function of chronological age. As we assess our fellows, we see every day people in their thirties, forties, and fifties who are no more mature than they were in their teens, and the tragedy of their lives is evident to everyone about them. More rarely, unfortunately, we see a few people who give positive evidence of being mature by the time they have finished high school, and these fortunate people have a tremendous advantage over their competitors on the job and in general living.

It is quite apparent that an adult's philosophy is not born full blown overnight. Plank by plank, it is hewn from our living from day to day, and the construction of each part is associated with a certain amount of trauma for the individual affected. We might illustrate this with an example concerning a young person who has never really stopped to examine his thinking about personal honesty. He has never been put into a situation which tempts him greatly, so how can he know what his reaction will be until that happens? When it does occur, and it will to everyone at some time, the outcome of his struggle will strongly shape his future. If he succumbs to temptation the first time, the way is clear for him to react dishonestly many more times, until a behavioral pattern is set for the rest of his life.

It is important to remind ourselves that the young and immature are notoriously selfish in their reactions. They analyze every situation immediately for what can be had to their advantage, rather than for what is best for the most, or at least for the group in which they are functioning. At the moment when a man or woman first starts to consider the welfare of others in deciding his or her actions, we know that person is well on the way to maturity, and can be expected to make a positive contribution to both the enterprise and society. This reaction often has some religious overtones, but it is not necessary for religion to play a part in the rational decision that others have some rights also. It will, in any case, be a strong plank in anyone's personal philosophy.

Another matter which will be decided by the maturation process is the way in which a person relates to those about him in purely interpersonal reactions. The effective manager is the one who has the best relationships with subordinates, just as long as there is no sacrifice of personal principle to maintain good feeling. The quicker anyone discovers that it is to his advantage to get along well on the whole with his associates, the quicker that person will realize solid success in his chosen work.

We should not be misled by the spectacular, but rare, exceptions to this principle. We can all name those who have great successes—for a time—while stepping all over those about them, but their numbers are so few as simply to reinforce the mathematical odds against such happenings in the world we live in. For every Hitler, Insull, or Kreuger the world has known, there have been hundreds of thousands of successful managers who have been decent in their overall relationships with their associates. Since most of us are average citizens in most respects, we should play the odds as they are in our favor, rather than deviate and take the chances of a tragic outcome to our careers. This decision is another milepost on the road to personal maturity.

The reader by this time may be aware that I have been strongly influenced in my thinking by Abraham Maslow and his humanistic philosophy. Maslow states several times in his writing that only the persons operating at level 5 of the "hierarchy of needs" (self-actualization) have good mental health. This means that these "metamotivations," as he calls them, must be the overriding "pushes" behind mature people in whatever mode of living they find themselves. Actually, they don't "find" themselves anywhere—they are the architects of their own fate and have a decisive influence on the course of their own lives and careers.

What we have indicated so far in this chapter is really a truism: Managers should be quick in starting to formulate their personal philosophies, since they cannot operate meaningfully on the job until this has been set in its original form. As we shall see a bit further downstream, this first personal philosophy will *not* be the final one; this fact should not militate against the first formulation, since it is absolutely necessary to getting off the ground.

To the nostalgic person of middle or advanced age, it may appear tragic that we recommend to young managers that they abandon the ways of youth and hasten the aging process. Actually, we are not really doing this. As stated before, maturation is not necessarily equated directly with age, and there is good argument to support the position that achieving a sound personal philosophy will help to keep us *younger* in our thinking and living. People who simply ride the stream without a sextant or a rudder may find themselves aging prematurely, without having anything significant behind them in the way of accomplishment. And these, indeed, are the pathetic figures in the world we live in.

PERSONAL PHILOSOPHY SHOULD AGREE WITH COMPANY PHILOSOPHY

Whatever direction the manager's personal philosophy takes, he or she is in big trouble unless it is generally congruent with the philosophy of the company. There is no role conflict more severe for managers than to work for a company whose overall philosophy is at variance with their own. For example, if you are a warm, outgoing person, you will find no lasting peace in an organization which shows very little concern for people. The first time, or the tenth time, that you see some person ground down and destroyed because the dictates of a hard-nosed company demand it, you will find yourself in a turmoil. By the same token, if you are a no-nonsense, hard-shelled person, you will find it intolerable if, in your thinking, the company continuously "coddles" its employees or is too permissive by your standards.

These untenable positions should be resolved at once, since it is both intellectually and physically taxing to go on working in this unfavorable sort of climate. If we were to take a good, hard look at things, we would probably discover that a large percentage of the stress and tension associated with a manager's work situation comes from this kind of dilemma.

Another area where conflict can arise is in fiscal policy. The manager who is by and large conservative in money matters will not be comfortable in a concern which plunges in and takes risks with big amounts of its capital. It leaves him with a sense of insecurity that is hard to live with. Conversely, if a manager is by nature a gambler, he will find the constraints of a conservative or reactionary company too galling to endure for long.

A third area which can cause trouble is managerial style.

This is, of course, the direct offspring of your personal philosophy. If, in your thinking, your sole objective as a manager is to make as much profit as you can for your employers, you will become task-oriented to the exclusion of any consideration of the people working for you, and your managerial style will be abrasive to the point where your people will hate and fear you.

If, with this managerial style, you find yourself in a concern where consideration for people is one of the fundamentals of the corporate philosophy, you will be continually at odds with higher management and will find yourself circumscribed beyond endurance. If you have found the compromising, middle-of-the-road style to be most effective for you, you will not operate well in a company which is demanding and hard-nosed. These people would see compromise as a sign of weakness in you, and their faith in your managerial ability would be eroded.

If you have strong convictions that a manager should have wide latitude to make decisions in his area of responsibility and are working for a company where everything is either done by the book or not done at all, you would again find yourself unable to function effectively. By the same token, if you look pretty much to upper management for guidance in strange situations, you would not be happy in a totally decentralized concern that expects you to make all your own decisions.

It is fairly obvious that in any of the situations cited above something is going to have to change. As we have seen, these things cannot be tolerated for long, either by the individual manager or by the company. If a long look at the situation convinces you that you cannot alter things so far as the company is concerned, and if you find it impossible to adjust your position, the only feasible alternative is to sever your connection with the enterprise.

On the other hand, as a manager, you should never underestimate your powers of persuasion and the influence you have with members of upper management. After all, they did select you for your position; they do have confidence in your judgment; you are a member of the management group. You owe it to yourself to have a run at changing the company's philosophy, if you are truly convinced that it is wrong, before calling off the deal. A little search may reveal other managers in your enterprise who share your convictions, and as a group you may have enough clout to swing the course around to what you feel to be suitable. This has happened many times before, and will again.

If your personal philosophy is still evolving, you should concentrate on making a real effort to mold it toward the general direction of the company's philosophy. As long as you go on working there, you should try hard to go with the guidelines your employer has laid down if at all possible.

This brings us back to the fact that it is your responsibility to be fully cognizant of the philosophy of your company. Your employers have a responsibility to communicate it to you, but you are the person who must eventually live with it, and this entails an active, ongoing effort to ensure that you are reading them correctly and that you know where they want to go. It is amazing how many enterprises ignore these basic essentials, with the result that the management group is individually and collectively flying by the seat of the pants. Anything felicitous coming from this can only be the wildest of chance.

Keeping a balance between your own philosophy and that of the company or agency for which you work is one of your continuing duties as a manager; it cannot be long from your mind if you are to keep a proper composure in your work situation.

PERSONAL PHILOSOPHY MUST BE SUBJECT TO CHANGE

We have just indicated one situation in which a manager's personal philosophy may have to change: when there is conflict between it and the company's philosophy. That is, the personal one must be changed if the manager wishes to remain where he or she has been, or the resultant role conflict will be too severe.

There are other factors which may call for an adjustment in personal philosophy. The most important of these relate to the massive changes occurring with such frightening rapidity in our culture. The only way to survive the total effects of these changes is to be flexible at all times. It is mandatory that we adjust as quickly as possible to a new situation which will have impact on our lives.

On the business and industrial scene, two changes are currently operative which will have an effect on the career of every manager in America. The first one is the EEO legislation at the national level. Those managers who relax and lie back, thinking that this is another token push by the Congress to fend off the needling of pressure groups, are in for a severe shock. It is becoming abundantly evident that this time tokenism will not do the trick. Businessmen everywhere are going to have to defend their actions in the areas of hiring and promoting many groups. Blacks and other ethnic minorities will have to be given equal treatment at last. Women in business have given notice that they will not be discriminated against any longer; they are ready to take whatever measures are necessary to assure themselves of equal pay for equal work, and they are determined to penetrate some fields which traditionally have been closed to them.

A second major hindrance is arising in the form of the national Occupational Safety and Health Act (OSHA). Under its present provisions, there is no business enterprise in the United States which would not be subject to citation by an OSHA inspector if he found something wrong. The structure set up by the enabling legislation has turned out regulations by the hundreds of thousands; a special school has been built to train inspectors in their incalculably complicated jobs.

So far, the reaction of businessmen and managers has been largely one of panic and blind fear. They have done almost everything except the one thing which is absolutely necessary; to change their personal and company philosophies to adjust to this new and better approach to business and industrial safety measures. We are about to see the passing of the days when a workman's health and even his life were of little or no concern to his employers. The control method will be the only one to which managements will respond: a threat to their financial safety. If they continue to disregard the requirements of OSHA, it is entirely possible that their fines could add up to bankruptcy.

Another strong reason for the manager to remain completely fluid in his or her personal thinking is an internalized one. All managers are aware of the fact (but some much more so than others) that to continue to be effective as managers they must continue to grow and develop as individuals. The day a manager ceases to grow and to learn more, his job is on the line and he is on the way out. The implication of this is, naturally, that the personal philosophy of a manager will grow and become more complex as he or she grows as a total individual. There would be no purpose, and no real good adduced, from growth as such unless the guidelines also grew to accommodate the new person.

In direct line with this reasoning, let it be stated that another reason for changing our personal philosophy is to reduce the internal struggles and resultant tensions while we are growing. Just as we had growing pains as adolescents, so we have trauma associated with our maturation and growth as adults. It is not an easy thing to mature. We are subjected to all the fears and worries about the unknown, and the new person emerging within us is truly unknown to us at first. We have to adjust our personal leadership methods just as we adjust those we use on our work force as it changes its form and nature. The thing is that our personal changes are harder to see, recognize, and categorize than those which are taking place in people about us. It is always harder to know ourselves than others.

Just as we are undergoing this constant change, so are those with whom we work. Granted, they will not always be growing in the same direction or to the same degree, but they will be different from what they were before, and this means that we have to be prepared to adjust to their new configurations. This is true of those who work for us, those who are our peers, and the line of management above us. Our response to these three groups of people will be quite different in each case, but the essential thing to remember is that *we must make a response*. They will expect it of us, just as we expect them to be aware of and to react to changes in us.

This is another iteration of the complexities of group living in today's society. Some of us can remember times when life was much simpler, when issues were delineated in stark blacks and whites. Those days are gone — probably forever in this society. It is not for us to argue here which is the better situation; what we have to do now is to adjust and to make the necessary changes in order to survive and prosper in *today's* world.

The process of making the necessary changes in our personal philosophy will be a repetition of the original process of giving it birth. Nothing new will be introduced in the methodology, and this should tend to reduce the pressure on us while we make the new adjustments. And we should be stimulated by pleasurable anticipation of a more effective set of personal directives for ordering our business lives.

PERSONAL PHILOSOPHY IS THE MANAGER'S CONSCIENCE

We have made the point previously that the development of a personal philosophy is a part of growing up — maturing — as an individual and as a manager. Also, we have posited that a personal philosophy must be generally in agreement with the philosophy of the enterprise if the manager is to be at ease with himself and his colleagues and that it must be subject to change under a changing mix in the surroundings faced by the manager. One more necessity must be faced by all of us as we live our business lives: Within the confines of our dealings with others at work, our personal philosophy must function as our conscience and our ethical guide.

The permissibility of a course of action is exceedingly difficult to determine in these days of explosive change and in the different subcultures which arise among us, with value sets and life styles often diametrically opposed to one another. What is perfectly acceptable in one group is totally objectionable in another; we have to make decisions for ourselves in these areas, even when we are dealing with others who have different values and different approaches to life.

If there is any one, unvarying premise on which we have to build our lives, it is that every manager has to develop a code of dealing with others which is not subject to negotiation so long as the personal philosophy involved is not changed in a major way. Our mental health is almost totally dependent upon maintaining this attitude and on pursuing a course of action completely in accord with our current personal philosophy. Pure chaos can be the only result if a group of managers plays every situation on a different ethical and moral basis; we cannot survive as a culture or a nation if this kind of operation runs rampant for even a few years.

The effects on us as individuals of a negation of this principle are fairly obvious. If we do not follow what we believe to be the right course of action, we will be punished—if not by others, then by ourselves. And self-punishment is always more severe and lasting than any which others might levy upon us. We can never run away from ourselves.

Another reason for using a purely personal philosophy as a conscience is that we can be sure that we will be much more committed to it than to any we might passively accept from others. It is for this reason that we must use our personal philosophy, and not that of our employers, as a measure of our personal behavior. It is entirely possible that our employers might countenance behavior unacceptable to us as individuals, and this is too trying a situation in which to operate. Of course, if these two variables bring us into direct conflict with our employers, we then have another, more fundamental decision to make. Surely, there must be another place to work if necessary.

At the same time, it is essential to let those about us know what our ethical beliefs call for in the way of business behavior. Just as we hate to operate in the dark with others, so our peers and those who report to us want to know what our principles are so that they won't be brought up short in dealing with us in any given situation.

We are talking here about the fundamental difference between reputation and character. In nearly every case they will reflect each other almost perfectly, but it could be possible in some situations that our public image will not exactly correspond to our real character. The discrepancy might go in either direction. That is, our basic character might be better or worse than the way those about us see us. In either case, it makes for difficult interactions with both individuals and groups if they see us as different from what we really are. Again, we can see the absolute necessity for good, clear, definitive communication with others about our personal philosophy and how it will affect our actions and reactions.

It is important to reinforce the matter discussed in the previous segment. There is absolutely nothing incongruous about saying that our personal philosophy will be our conscience and at the same time recognizing that our philosophy will be subject to constant change. Hopefully, those changes will be of an evolutionary nature and will result in our becoming bigger and better people with each major step. In other words, we will be operating more and more in the area of Maslovian self-actualization, which, according to Maslow, all people with good mental health are working for most of the time. So long as the change in our thinking is the result of personal growth and refinement, we have nothing to worry about.

The fact that so much has been made here of our personal involvement in building a personal philosophy in no way negates the possibility of others having great influence on the way we go. In fact, we could hold a good brief for the generalization that no one can evolve as good a philosophy alone as he could if he listened to and considered the inputs of others. The trick is to listen to the right people while we are building a philosophy for ourselves.

3

THE RESPONSIBILITIES OF A MANAGER

The subject of managerial responsibility becomes a little gray when we consider that there are some generic responsibilities which every manager assumes and which only part of the group of managers pays any attention to. Then there are responsibilities which are imposed on managers by the enterprise and which vary widely, in some cases being entirely antithetical from company to company. Overall, we are concerned philosophically with three basic kinds of managerial responsibilities: technical, human, and conceptual responsibilities. These duties can never be escaped or delegated away; they are with the manager so long as he remains in a managerial position.

TECHNICAL RESPONSIBILITIES

Managers at every level have technical responsibilities toward their people and the work they do. However, it is obvious that the first and second levels of management are much more deeply embroiled in the technical side of the job than are managers further up the hierarchy. This is because interleafing of more levels of management removes the higher managers from direct contact with the people who do the work. As we are all aware, if a manager stays away from new development in his technical field for even a few years, he becomes obsolescent in the discipline. The half-life of an engineer is now said to be five years, unless the engineer makes a serious and formal effort to keep up with new developments in the field.

The group leader at the first level of management will have to remain a resource person for his employees when they have technical problems. Unless they can go to the boss with their troubles and receive some aid and comfort, they will lose every vestige of respect for their managers. Naturally, it would be ridiculous to expect that the supervisor will have an immediate answer to every technical question which may arise, but he or she must at least know where to get that immediate answer, and it goes without saying that speed is of the essence in these situations.

It should be evident that there will be times when the manager will deliberately *not* give the answer immediately, even if he has it at his fingertips. If there is reason to suspect that a worker is goldbricking or just going for a ride on the back of a boss who is an easy mark, he should be brought up short and shown at once that he has some responsibility too. But it may be the considered judgment of the boss that here is a learning opportunity for the worker which cannot be duplicated in any other way, and he may decide to let the subordinate find out for himself or herself. Lessons learned that way usually stick.

It must be remembered that those in higher management will still have a deep interest in what is going on technically on the floor or in the office. They will never lose this interest, since the technical side of the business, whatever it is, will always be of the utmost importance to its success. As noted earlier, those managers three or more steps up the ladder will probably become obsolescent in their discipline as they become more deeply involved in management itself. The way to handle this dilemma, and the approach usually taken, is for managers at these levels to hire out their technical questions. In order for this to be successful, there must be trust and confidence of the highest order between the technician and the manager.

Another point to be gotten across at the earliest moment is that the responsibilities of the technician stop short of making managerial decisions. His position is purely staff;

decisions remain the job of the manager in this kind of relationship. The manager will find it impossible to make good decisions unless he has good technical information; but once this has been acquired, he carries the responsibility for deciding which way to go at a crossroad, and any staff people working for him must be made to understand this as a part of their job orientation.

There is another facet of technical responsibility which must be explored. This is the fact that in many industries today the first-line supervisor is leading representatives of several skills or crafts, yet there is no possible chance that he will be expert in all of them. A good example is the supervisor in final assembly of the airframe industry. He is normally responsible for such combinations of skills as carpenters, electricians, plumbers, sheet-metal workers, upholsterers, painters, sealers, and perhaps even others.

Naturally, no one could expect this supervisor to be a journeyman in all these skills. It is incumbent upon him, however, to get the basic knowledge in each skill which will enable him to tell when the work turned out is acceptable and when it is not. In other words, the supervisor must have enough expertise in all areas to direct the work effectively and to maintain proper control over the flow of the job.

Management people must be aware of these changing demands upon them for technical knowledge as they rise in the hierarchy. They will then be required to adjust their behavior to the level occupied by them at a given time. If it is apparent that the actual job of managing is becoming more important to them personally than keeping up with their technical skills, they should gracefully retire from their background discipline, hire technicians, and devote their time and energies to becoming more effective as managers — which is, after all, the job for which they now draw their paychecks.

HUMAN RESPONSIBILITIES

Until relatively few years ago, management at large simply refused to admit the existence of any responsibility toward the human element of the enterprise. Working people were looked upon just as any other tools or machinery used to make the product, and they were expected to fend for themselves, on the job as well as off. Safety records were abominable; employees who were injured or who contracted job-related illnesses were given short shrift when they became unable to work any longer. Even after employers were forced by law to start providing some basic safety precautions and to be liable for financial protection, there was only a minuscule realization of any real duty toward the men and women whose labors made it possible for the owners to make a profit.

Actually, it has been largely since the penetration of the behavioral scientists into business and industry that managers have come to realize that in the long run they will profit from having a healthy and reasonably happy group of people working for them. The tide of thinking in this area was turned with the completion of the Hawthorne Study in the 1930s. True, at first there was an overreaction, with a resultant two decades or so of fatuous thinking in which "human relations" was God, managers believed that all they had to do to be successful was to "human relate" at a high level of competency, and "fire" was a nasty word.

As might be expected, when the fallacy of this position was universally recognized the pendulum swung back the other way, and we are once again seeing a much harder attitude toward employees on the part of some managers. The difference is that in the meantime labor organized and entrenched its position so deeply that it is no longer possible for an employer to exploit his people for any significant length of time. He will be quickly caught up and brought into line by both the might of the unions and the courts of the land.

Over and above this simple set of circumstances, there is beginning to flow in the consciousness of American management a belief that businesses *do* have some basic and inescapable responsibilities toward the people who work for them. Many little details reveal the growth of this facet of managerial philosophy. Witness the diminution of managerial resistance toward the idea of decent sick-leave and vacation policies, to be incorporated into a sane kind of retirement policy after a reasonable period of service to the company.

Above and beyond these rather cold and impersonal generalities are appearing some much more human considerations. It is no longer the exceptional company that has a stated policy and set of activities to prepare the aging employee for the impact of retirement. Some managers still hate to admit it, but it is implicit in the job of the leader to assume the position of a parent figure to those in the work group — irrespective of the chronological ages of the leader and the followers.

In other words, no matter how much it may add to the already heavy load of the manager, he will be required to be as responsive as he can to any cue from an employee that he has problems he would like to discuss with his supervisor. It is highly probable that the manager will not be equipped or trained to handle this problem on a personal basis, and it may have to be referred. But the important point is that the leader recognize his fundamental duty to respond to a call for help and be available at all times as a catalyst to get something started.

As a manager rises in the hierarchy, this outlook toward people undergoes a curious but logical change. The supervisor at the first or second level has a very personal approach to his duties to people; he thinks of them in terms of the Joes and Marys who work for him. After a promotion or two, these social responsibilities become more generalized. The individual faces may tend to become a little blurred, while "people thinking" will be blended with the increased financial burdens put upon the organization as a result of these newly recognized obligations. As our society becomes more complex and demanding, more monies are going into the financial planning of a business to take care of the proliferating needs and expectations of the working public. This is a managerial responsibility that can never again be evaded or ignored.

Nothing in this writing should be construed as support for a soft or coddling attitude toward the employee on the part of management. It should be simple recognition of the fact that the employment bargain is a two-way road: The employee owes his employer a full day's work of high quality; the employer owes the employee decent pay and adequate fringe benefits for value received.

In this area as nowhere else it is of fundamental importance that support for a humanistic approach to employees be unbroken at every level of management. If first, second, or third levels of management are supportive of this philosophy but middle and top echelons negate this thinking, nothing will result. Conversely, if top management are people of good will but the layers below them in the hierarchy do not go along, even the most advanced policies and procedures for employees will be lost and not implemented. In this one area there *must* be absolute consensus.

CONCEPTUAL RESPONSIBILITIES

At the first or second level of management there is little need for conceptual skill inherent in the job. In fact, in some organizations the first two levels of managers are strongly discouraged from exercising any conceptual skills, since this can interfere with the plans made by middle management and executives. Nevertheless, any person intending to make a career in management should exercise whatever skill he or she possesses in "painting with a broad brush" and in "seeing the big picture." This is so that when advancement has been made to the levels where conceptualization is required as a part of the job, the manager will be ready to perform this function properly.

The manager charged with conceptualizing the changes necessary for an enterprise to remain competitive must remember that this duty has several facets. The first is to determine in what new direction or directions the firm should be going in the next few years. Today very few businesses can remain static in either product mix or services rendered for more than a few years if they hope to survive. Obviously, it is going to be up to management personnel to determine these new directions, communicate them to others in the enterprise, convince them of the necessity for change, and then implement the changes at the proper times. It is for this reason that every manager, irrespective of the discipline in which he is employed, must keep close liaison with research and development within the organization. Not only must he be aware of what is going on there; he must stand ready at all times to make proper inputs of his own if ideas occur which seem worthy of following up.

The second facet of this responsibility is to do whatever market research may be necessary to ensure that a planned product or service will be accepted by customers if it is put into the company's catalogue. It is seldom possible to depend on managerial intuition in this respect; there must be some good, solid work done in advance of committing the company's resources to a new venture, no matter how glittering the idea may seem on paper.

The next major facet of the manager's conceptual responsibility is to make sure that company personnel are kept up to date and ready for changes as they become necessary or desirable. In other words, the people needs of the enterprise will change just as drastically and just as fast as will the needs for new products or services. This does not necessarily mean that there will be changes in personnel; rather, the personnel will be changed by training or further education so that they will be ready for the new factors and ways of doing things.

In fact, the modern manager does less than his full job in this area if he fails to establish a timetable for the growth and development of all his people, and most certainly for himself as well. If one of his bright young people is now twenty-five, with a good education and lots of drive, the manager must be able to conceptualize what that person will be like in education and skills ten years from now, and fifteen years, and twenty years. These growth needs must also be communicated to the employee in question, so that he can be prepared for the necessary efforts to accomplish this tailored growth on schedule.

It is entirely probable that in conceptualizing what the company will be doing five or ten years from now the manager will discover that there will be needs for personnel not now in the employ of the company. Maybe some entirely new disciplines will be needed; the manager must be ready with a plan and timetable for bringing these new people aboard and welding them into the organization as productive members at exactly the right moment.

In his conceptualizing duties, the manager cannot forget for long that changes already contemplated or underway might alter the entire organizational structure. Perhaps it is time to drop the traditional pyramidal structure and change over to the matrix type of organization which is proving effective in so many businesses today. The more complex the business, the more likely that the matrix organization will be useful in reducing the uncertainties of operation. This sort of changeover is harrowing and must be well planned and executed.

A final facet of the manager's conceptual responsibility is the financial planning which will be necessary to carry out any expected changes. Almost all business changes today require huge amounts of new capital or else entail tying up for long periods capital already available within the organization. The manager does not have to be a financial specialist in order to get into this part of the act, but he most certainly will need the advice and counsel of experts in the field to be sure that he is doing his homework properly.

In summary, the conceptualization necessary for a manager could be called intelligent, planned dreaming. This skill is not congenital; it has to be cultivated assiduously by the individual, and will require much practice before adeptness is achieved. It should also be remembered that the smart manager will cultivate several resource people to help him gain skill in this area. It is always a good practice to have available one or more "wise old heads" with whom to interact when an idea is being gestated. This interaction is often profitable during a discussion of plans for new things.

4

THE MANAGER
AND INNOVATION

The American concept of management has always contained the elements of giving birth to and tending the process of change in the business and industrial scene. Unless we have continuous change, we shall stagnate and die. Where we have sometimes gone astray is in engendering change so rapidly that we have not had the time to fit it into our lives as individuals and groups of workers. This is one of the more important unmet challenges today in the field of management, and one on which we must work hard.

THE LEADER MUST LEAD

One of the reasons management has failed to meet this challenge is the widespread reluctance of nominal managers and leaders to accept the responsibility of leading the work force in a positive, firm manner toward reasoned and communicated goals. We are nearly forced to feel that part of this failure of today's manager is a fallout of two things: the youth itself of many of our designated leaders, plus the fact that the permissiveness of their upbringing has bypassed a necessary inculcation of the acceptance of responsibility.

I had a personal experience which helped me gain insight into this problem about three years ago. My wife and I were having cocktails at a small, favorite restaurant near our home. Just as we were about to go in to dinner, some forty young men came boiling up from a banquet room in the basement of the restaurant and invaded the bar. We discovered that this was the initiation banquet for that year's crop of pledges. We spent nearly three hours in conversation with this fine group of young men, and there was one inescapable conclusion from our extended interaction with them. Every single one of them expressed, either overtly or tacitly, a need for something which had been lacking in their lives: No one had ever disciplined them. They were vehement in their upset and irritation at this lack in their upbringing. This is not to say for a moment that they would have accepted the yoke of self-discipline without question, but there could be no question about their need for discipline.

When people of this sort first enter business and industry, and especially when they are tabbed for supervisory or managerial positions, this basic defect becomes glaringly apparent and also appears to the young men and women as a major threat both to their success as managers and to their security as human beings in the working world. The rest of management then is under the obligation of filling in this void in the early training of these people; if they have never had it before, the least managers can do is to chink up the holes in their armor and make them competitive with their peers.

One of the principal reasons for the hesitancy of the young manager to take on a position of leadership is the age inversion which occurs so often when a young leader takes over. He will probably find himself supervising several people (perhaps even a majority of his group) who are older than he is. Naturally, this gives rise to trepidation and insecurity on his part. Of course, there may be some basis in truth for his fears; older workers may refuse to accept, at least at first, the leadership of the youthful manager. It will be much harder for him to establish a position of clear and effective leadership with this handicap hanging over him.

Under these circumstances, it becomes abundantly evident that there is a critical need for ongoing leadership training for the entry-level manager — and this may have to be extended into middle management as well. When the basics have been omitted, the finer nuances have no foundation on which to be attached. Management training in the United States is making some important breakthroughs. For almost twenty-five years after the initial penetration of the behavioral scientists into the management field, progress was agonizingly slow. But in the past fifteen years we have seen a proliferation of the contributions made by behaviorists to effective management practice. Now there are relatively few businessmen and executives who have not accepted the contributions of behavioral science to business success.

At the same time, there have been enormous gains on the technical side of management. We are approaching the time when we can say that we are managing the computer, rather than being its slave. Operations Research (Management Science) has been refined to the point where it is an efficient and trusted tool in managerial decision making.

What the individual manager has to do, then, is fairly clear. After the initial acceptance of the responsibility for leadership, which as we have seen may not come easily, the manager must take the reins and guide his team toward successfully meeting organizational goals. The great majority of working people are happier as followers than they would ever be as leaders, but they are intensely unhappy and fearful if they see their nominal leaders refuse to accept, or at least dodge, the mantle of leadership and its attendant responsibilities and hard work.

The leader must lead. Unless we all accept this truism, we are in for a hard session in our business and industrial operations, and the prognosis is not very good. However, on the hopeful side, every day we see indications that new managers, after an understandable period of vacillation, *are* accepting this part of their total responsibility and are buckling down to meet new situations with every sign of eventual success.

TREND SENSING

To be a manager today, one must be at the head of the group in sensing what is about to happen just a tiny bit before it occurs. One small-town druggist made a fortune by having an intuitive sense of what was about to be "in" with his customers. For example, in the early 1920s, musical powder boxes were extremely popular. Then they dropped from sight, and people stored them away lest they be thought unfashionable by their friends. One day in the mid-1930s the druggist was talking with a jobber about his purchases for the coming Christmas season. The jobber laughingly said that he was stuck with 150 musical powder boxes he was unable to unload anywhere. Instantly the druggist made him an offer for the lot, and the jobber accepted.

During the Christmas shopping season the druggist sold every one of the boxes and could have sold many more. He was unable to explain what had made him buy them, except that they were pretty and, for the times, a novelty. If this had been a unique experience in the life of the druggist it could have been written off as a lucky chance, but he did this sort of thing throughout his business career, until his competitors started to watch what he was doing so they could emulate him. Their problem was that by the time they had determined his course he had changed direction, and they never quite caught up with his maneuverings.

As stated a moment ago, any manager who wants to be a real success today has to cultivate an intuitive sense of direction of change of the business world. The methodology for doing this is relatively simple to describe but very hard to implement consistently. Essentially, the manager must continually take a random sampling of what is going on about him, evaluate these events, sort them mentally, and be prepared to draw logical conclusions from this body of data. The catch is that he must consistently do this faster than others about him; this faculty, when developed, will add materially to his leadership of his people and will gain him the respect of other managers.

The advantages of competency in trend sensing are obvious. The manager who can foresee a change in the business world which will affect him can plan ahead for the changes he must make and will have enough leadtime to prepare for a different operation without throwing everyone into a panic. There will often be monetary advantages as well, in the way of getting materials or equipment before prices go up as they become in short supply.

One of the more visible of the bad effects of *not* being able to sense trends is what happened to the women's clothing industry a few years back. For many years clothing firms had been accustomed to declaring by fiat what women would wear, and whatever they put on sale became the mode of the moment. However, they failed to sense the reaction of the public when they introduced the "midi." Women rebelled and refused to wear what was to have been the coming style. The losses to the trade ran into the billions, including the failure of many women's wear firms that had invested most of their net worth in the midi style. This happening is far from unique. There have been thousands of similar situations in many kinds of business which were not so spectacular but which had just as devastating an effect on the people who failed to sense a coming trend.

The manager cannot afford to have tunnel vision in this area. If he concentrates solely on his own business and industry, he may fail to see what is going on elsewhere, and this will eventually have an impact on his business. The people in the light-metals industry most certainly should be interested in new developments in plastics, since the latter have already made significant inroads in areas where aluminum once was top dog. This kind of example could be multiplied by the thousands throughout the industrial world.

The manager should never depend soley on his personal resources in practicing the fine art of trend sensing. The quicker he can build up a stable of "stringer" correspondents, the quicker he will become adept at this part of his job. The people in his own work group, his peers, his friends in other businesses—anyone with whom his relations are good—can become a valuable source cf information about what is going on. The point is that they have to be alerted to the need and become accustomed to performing this friendly service on an ongoing basis. Naturally, the manager becomes indebted to these people, but it is the sort of obligation which is both easy and pleasurable to repay in many little ways throughout the years.

We have been describing here a characteristic which not all managers possess, or at least which not all have cultivated adequately. Unfortunately, in the immediate future these managers may find themselves expendable unless they mend their ways and start to work on developing this managerial tool quickly and effectively. As the position of manager comes closer and closer to being a profession, we must be aware of many little refinements in the job, each of which may not be a make-or-break situation but which in the aggregate most certainly will determine the effectiveness of any given manager.

We have definitely left behind us the day when managers could navigate by the seat of their pants. World War I airplanes were flown by dashing and glamorous heroes with goggles and neck scarves; the 747 is actually flown by a small computer, with a human pilot to check its activities and to take over in an emergency. The scene in modern business managership is quite analogous to these changes in flying over the past fifty years. The main difference is that radical changes in the job of the manager will occur infinitely more quickly than in the illustration just cited. Today we have to be quick to stay alive!

TREND MAKING

Even more essential than trend sensing to a truly successful career as a manager is the achievement of enough influence and prestige to have a say about the formation of new trends. The management of innovation has as one part of its conceptual framework that the manager will create many new things in his career. Some of these will be minor and rather inconsequential, but it is probable that every manager who remains in the field for a lifetime will have one or several major developments to his credit. As these achieve success, the responsible manager will begin to be regarded as a moving influence in his industry or service field.

For example, one purchasing director of a large corporation conceived the brilliant idea of attaching a draft to the bottom of his company's purchase orders. When the order was filled, the vendor completed the draft for the correct amount and returned it to the company for his money. The savings during the first year were in the hundreds of thousands of dollars. At first the system was limited to small purchases, but as its success became manifest it was extended to larger and larger orders. The percentage of loss through fraud was minuscule and certainly never approximated the extra processing costs which had been necessary under the old billing system.

We are ready to grant that innate creativity varies widely from person to person, but there can be no question that this is an art which can be acquired and cultivated by a person who realizes the importance of innovation and creativity in his work. As much as anything else, this special activity is the result of a frame of mind. The manager who is constantly on the lookout for the relationships between events, for the causes and effects of things that happen, will soon come to see the necessary rearrangements and alterations which will produce something new.

The innovative manager will come to have a new concept of spatial relations. Physical rearrangement of the same elements will many times result in a valuable change in a manufacturing process. Slight variations in layout have been known to result in huge savings. At the same time, no manufacturing process should ever be considered as sacred. The Bayer process for reducing bauxite to alumina in the aluminum industry went completely unchanged for nearly a century, but there was a fairly large and strong research team doing work on the process as recently as 1962. The fact that it had been unchanged for almost a hundred years did not mean that it couldn't be changed overnight if a new shortcut or refinement were discovered.

There are companies which come to hang their entire reputations (and a considerable amount of their sales) on their ability to be consistently innovative in their industry. IBM became a colossus because the business world started to look to it for what was new in electronic data processing. By the time some of the newer and smaller companies began to come out with important new products, IBM was so huge that it had an almost insuperable advantage over smaller competitors.

Many managers remain fat, dumb, and happy in their belief that this aspect of the business world is the domain and responsibility of the research and development groups and that the average manager has no duty in this area. Nothing could be more fallacious than a belief of this kind. The research and development groups in any enterprise should be the resource people and the staff for the line management. *Their function should be to process the ideas that come to them from the people who are directly responsible for getting the work done.* Two-way communication should be the premier objective of every department in its dealings with research groups. Sadly, in many companies this is not the case, with the result that research people are working in a vacuum, and even if they do come up with a spectacular potential winner, it may die for lack of understanding by the rest of the organization.

The trend maker in any company will have high status and the complete respect of other managers. Leadership of one's own people is a given in the thinking of management personnel; leadership of one's peers is a high accolade which all managers are constantly seeking. Trend making is one of the easier ways to get this leadership.

It should be amply evident that this is another part of the manager's job which cannot be done single-handedly. The manager who makes the trends will have received inputs from many people and from many situations. He or she will be faced with the constant necessity of going to resource people in many fields and disciplines for expert advice and counsel. In many cases there are esoteric necessities such as market research and field testing of products before they are released for mass production and national sales.

The manager who wants to become good at innovation and trend making should count himself fortunate if he is in a highly competitive industry. It is a fundamental psychological fact that managers who have little competition become complacent and will not consider the effort necessary to be innovative a requirement in their work. On the other hand, when managers know that half a dozen fierce competitors are right on their back, their responses will become much quicker and more accurate. Survival will be the garland for those who remember these ultimate facts of the real world.

JUDGMENTAL PROCESSES AND INNOVATION

The process of innovation brings to bear one of the heavier tests of the judgment of the manager. In considering the possibility of putting a new process, procedure, or methodology into an organization, the manager must make value judgments and comparisons at every step. What makes this doubly difficult is that in much of the way toward the establishment of the new there will be no historical guideposts against which to regard the proposal. What is proposed has never been done before, so how can the manager make anything but an educated guess in judging how to go?

There are, however, some basics which will help in this situation. To begin with, the manager does have voluminous data about what has been done traditionally. The good and weak points of the methodology will be clearly delineated and will suggest ways in which improvement is desirable. If these are pinpointed, the job of the manager then becomes one of designing improvements whose sole purpose is to do a better job than has been done before. Inherent weaknesses will be worked out of the planning job; demonstrated strengths will be worked in and maximized in the new design. It will be possible in most instances to do step testing of components and subassemblies before the new creation has been completely assembled. The aerospace industry has operated in this manner ever since its inception, and it is, of course, almost totally concerned with innovation at every step of the way.

One important aspect of the manager's judgment in innova-

tion is with the people concerned. Not everyone is so struc-
tured as to be adaptable to operating comfortably in a new
environment. Even if a person might eventually be able to
change his ways, it might take such a long time that the manager would do better to defer that person's assignment until
after the project has been well established and is running
smoothly. On the other hand, there are people who are most
comfortable in a situation of change. These are the ones who
find their job challenge in meeting the unexpected and in
making a new thing work. They are by far a minority of the
working population, but whenever identified they can do a
tremendous job in implementing innovation.

The manager of innovation must make many crucial judgments about his communications. Starting with his own management up the line, he must do a strong selling job on trying
the new idea. This communication can make or break the entire project. Communications with subordinates must be
delicately handled, with consummate timing, or the manager
will not have them with him and the idea will fail. In almost
every case, too, communications with peers must be at least as
delicate, because somewhere along the line the manager is
going to need their cooperation and goodwill if the new idea is
to succeed.

Outside contacts are equally important. If the innovation is
a new product, the manager must bring customers into the
scene at an early date, both to sell them on the desirability
of the new item and to give them time to adjust their inventories
in preparation for the new product. Similarly, vendors must
be talked to early so that they can prepare for any new items
which will be required in manufacturing the new product. One
of the judgments required of the manager may well be that of
looking for a new vendor or vendors if the old ones fail to
measure up to the new demands.

Another critical demand on the judgmental ability of the
manager is in the overall timing involved. There is always a
right time and a wrong time to propose change. Perhaps the
cash flow of the organization is under stress at the moment, for
whatever reason. It would not be politic to come forth at this

time with a proposal for a large capital expenditure to get the new idea off and flying. Or perhaps the local labor market is exceptionally tight at this time, and it is evident that the innovation will require some new skills and a number of new people. The prudent manager will consider these items in his planning. Possibly major changes have occurred in the top echelons of the company, and it is not yet clear whether there has been a major shift in managerial philosophy. It might be better to wait for a definition of this area before going upstairs with a major proposal for change. Again, this is up to the discretion of the manager.

Over and above all these elements, and the multitude of others not discussed, there is one factor in innovation which the manager can never ignore. Eventually, he will come to that area of penetration of the new field where there are no bases on which to make a valid judgment. It is at this point that the manager must fall back on intuition and hope that things will go his way.

The importance of intuitive processes in the work of a modern manager can hardly be overstated. No matter how careful and scientific we try to be, change is so rapid today in so many areas of our lives that we must stand ready to make decisions that are not always based on a full data bank of replicable figures. Therefore, the manager will be forced to fall back on his noninferential knowledge and fire away. Of course, this knowledge is the product of much experience which has been carefully analyzed and classified. What we are really talking about is making *innovative* use of what has happened to us before. If our heads are functioning properly, there is better than a reasonable chance that our intuition will counsel us wisely in making these necessary judgments in innovation.

IMPLEMENTATION OF CHANGE

Much has been written on the implementation of change, but this remains one of the larger and more troublesome problems facing a manager. Looking back for a moment at the opening segment of this chapter, we can find the key to getting innovation off the ground satisfactorily: The leader must lead. There must be strength and inspiration in the leadership of the group, since followers will naturally have their misgivings and will feel threatened at the prospect of the unknown. In the final analysis, change will be successfully instituted only when subordinates have enough faith and trust in the leadership to overcome their fears and doubts.

Previous to this, of course, the manager must reassure himself that the course proposed has a reasonable chance of succeeding. That is, he must overcome his own fears and doubts about what he is asking the group to do. It is a widely held misconception that all leaders have innate self-confidence in every situation they face. Nothing could be further from the truth. High among the hazards of managership is the continuous stress placed on the manager to succeed; he or she most certainly will know how many factors can go wrong and cause trouble in the implementation of change. Obviously, the cure for these fears will be a succession of successful ventures into the unknown. If the leader can look back with satisfaction on getting three or four new things safely off the ground, he will have much more confidence the next time he faces the task of persuading his people to go along with him into the unknown.

On the part of the followers, fear of change may have its basis in several factors. High among them is uncertainty as to what will happen to them in the new setup. There may be strong feelings of inadequacy, plus a belief that the new training involved may be too much for them. This is especially true of older employees who have been away from the "school" situation for a long time. The leader must recognize this possibility and immediately take steps to allay these doubts and to convince his people that they can overcome the difficulties inherent in the proposed changes. Constant reiteration of the leader's belief in his people is the best medicine for this group illness.

Another very cogent reason for resistance to change on the part of the work force is the fear of a reduction in status under the new system, either within the group or throughout the organization. Here again, the leader holds the only release from this quite natural mental distress. The employee has worked for months or years in one job and has spent a considerable amount of time and effort building a role for himself in the organization. This self-image is a product of his own efforts plus the reinforcement given to him by his peers and his management. If the proposed change gives him the idea that his position in the group will be threatened, his reaction will be heavily negative—perhaps even to the point of causing him to try to sabotage the proposal.

It must be admitted that sometimes a new method does result in this lowering of status. If this is in the package, the manager probably would do better to find a new spot for the people involved and then reman the organization with people from other areas who would gain rather than lose status in the new job. This is not the time or place to go through an exhaustive examination of the many reasons why people try to avoid change, but the ones mentioned are typical and suggestive of the others. The principal purpose here is to alert the manager to his duties.

Overall, the manager must constantly be aware of the supreme importance of doing his homework before launching an innovation. His planning must be meticulous and complete, and he must allow for every possible alternative on both the "thing" and the "people" sides of the problem. A major alteration could easily require several months or years of planning before the manager can safely come to the implementation stage. The key to success in this part of the venture is to involve as many others as possible. The quicker this deep involvement is accomplished, the quicker doubts and fears will subside, with resultant positive attitudes on the part of everyone toward the new idea. In addition, the manager will almost certainly pick up some helpful new views.

Careful planning will help the manager avert another grave booby trap; the possibility of errors in logistics which might be fatal to the entire plan. It is imperative in starting up a new project that men, materials, and machines all be at the right place at the right time. Hundreds of well-conceived plans have gone down the drain because something wasn't where it should have been at a crucial moment in the flow.

The implication here is that there is no other situation in the manager's work life in which a good team effort is more important than in the implementation of a desired change. One thing is most certainly true: The manager can't do it by himself, and he is going to need the all-out cooperation of everyone in his group, plus many outsiders, to have a successful conclusion to his venture. This is one more reinforcement of the importance of interpersonal relationships for any manager. It seems incredible in view of this self-evident truth that so many American managers fail every year because they have not built and maintained viable relationships with those about them.

This is in no sense an indication that the manager must be weak or wishy-washy in order to get the goodwill of his fellows at work. Rather, it means ultimately that he must be *honest* and that his communications must be clear and complete. If employees come to know that they can trust—and understand—a given manager, the leader will have few problems with people on the job. This will be especially noticeable when change is the order of the day.

This chapter has been concerned with one of the most important and frequently arising situations in the modern manager's job. Change is happening all about us; if it doesn't happen *to* us, we must often be under the charge of making it happen to others. In either event, the manager will be the fulcrum of the action, and he must have his ducks in a row before he begins.

5

THE MANAGER AS A CENSOR

Among the many tasks a manager assumes when he accepts his job is that of acting as a censor for his group. This judgmental activity will be concerned with actions, communications, and decisions and will go on in all the functions of management with which the leader is involved. Because of the nature of this activity, the manager will find his decisions sometimes leading to abrasive interpersonal reactions, since he will from time to time be obliged to deny favorite actions on the part of his people or else force them to do something which is unpopular. We shall speak of this matter more fully in the last segment of the chapter.

THE MONITORING PROCESS

The function of censor is of extreme importance to the success or failure of the manager. The temptation is always there to ease up on this responsibility just a little, in the vain and delusive hope that a bit of relaxation here will lead to greater popularity with subordinates. Actually, they will certainly see what is going on, and their opinion of the leader will suffer as they sense a continuing dereliction of important duty. Therefore, the manager will be doing no favor either to himself or to his people by not facing up to the unceasing demands in this area.

If we look first at monitoring activities in the communications of the group, we are immediately faced with one of management's oldest and most worrisome problems: what to tell, or not tell, its people. At the very outset, let us establish the inescapable fact that managers as a group are much more prone to keep back needed information than to pass it along. In some organizations this is carried to a ridiculous extreme, with the result that many of the troops are working completely in the dark, without enough information to get their work done. If carried on for long, this can kill an enterprise, and most certainly has in innumerable cases throughout the country.

In the matter of communication the manager has an individual responsibility second to none: *If he can determine no valid reason for withholding information, it should be passed on.* This attitude in itself will result in a significant increase in the amount of downward communication. The equal and opposite reaction will be just as meaningful: an increase in upward communication from the line where the action is really taking place.

We would certainly be remiss if we were to leave the inference that all information must be shared with everyone in the organization immediately. Most assuredly, there are many times when information should be restricted to only one or two echelons of management. These situations usually arise during the planning of a new venture, when indiscriminate release of information might result in its falling into the hands of competitors, with a resultant disadvantage to the home team.

The manager at each level should be in the best position to know whether to share a certain bit of news with his subordinates. In the first place, he knows his people better than anyone else and should be able to forecast their reactions to the news in question. The impetus from this nugget might be just what is required to get the team going to complete the new job. On the other hand, the information might pose a threat to key people in the group, in which case the manager should most certainly withhold the news until a more appropriate time.

The most difficult job in managerial censoring is to keep the information from *looking* too censored. If the gaps from the scissors are too obvious, people will be frustrated and angry at what they consider being treated like children. Of course, the manager knows best, and maybe some of his people are still infantile in their reactions. If this is the case, a little censorship may be the only possible answer.

Another area which has given managers more headaches than they can cure is the matter of individual behavior regarding dress. A few years ago there was little difficulty in establishing and maintaining dress codes in an organization; today it is nearly an impossibility, unless matters of safety or health can be brought in and substantiated. Today many employees, especially the younger ones, equate their identity with their manner of dress and regard any attempt to curb or change their actions as a threat to their personal freedom.

Once again, we are forced to ask ourselves whether management's actions in the matter of dress have always been reasonable or even useful. In many cases they seem in retrospect to have been whimsical and arbitrary in the extreme and to have served no real purpose except to alienate employees. The touchiest area of all is to try to impose and enforce a dress code under the pretext of having to be aware of the customer's reaction. Of course, public relations are important to every business concern, but we have often overreacted in hysteria to a paranoid fear of how the customer might respond.

Nevertheless, the onus of this responsibility is constantly with us as managers, and we will never be able to shuck it. Even though we may feel we are going to lose a round before the bell rings, our duty is still plainly to act as censors when our good sense tells us to do so. Assuredly, we won't win them all, but neither will we lose them all, and every one that we win will strengthen our position with our people and solidify our leadership within the organization.

JUDGING THE EFFECTIVENESS OF ACTIONS

It is entirely human to look immediately for an outside cause when some action we have taken proves to be wrong. Why should we assume the blame for the consequences if we can shift it to some other person or to a malfunctioning "thing"? However, every manager knows deep inside that this is *not* the way to do it. We have to be responsible in the long run for the messes we make, if for no other reason than to give us some assurance that we won't make the same kind of mistake again.

There are essentially only two kinds of mistakes a manager can make in handling his job: He can lack enough technical knowledge of the process—or of changes proposed—and thereby make a procedural error in judgment, or he can make mistakes with people in his interpersonal reactions with them. The "thing" mistakes can, of course, be very costly. However, as a manager rises in the hierarchy, and as the years go by, he will find himself becoming obsolescent in the specialty by which he got himself into management in the first place. It is inevitable that eventually he must lay aside any pretense at real technical expertise and depend on the judgments of the technical people he has hired to relieve him of this part of the job.

At the same time, the manager must be aware that in this action he has in no way escaped accountability for this part of his managerial function. If anything goes wrong technically through mistakes by his technical assistants, the manager is still totally responsible for what has happened. This means that the manager must constantly review what is going on with his technical people. *They are responsible only for technical aspects of the job.* Anything that happens as a result of technical actions is the sole responsibility of the manager in charge, and it is here that he must make many value judgments as the job proceeds toward conclusion.

What we have been saying is that the manager must be ready to censor the actions of his technical people the moment he has any reason to question the viability of a proposed course of action. It may be the manager cannot be sure that the proposal is wrong; it is still his duty to hold up proceedings until his people have convinced him they are right. More than that, they will have to do it by facts and figures which are understandable to him. Never could the manager be condoned for taking the unbacked word of one of his people if a question has arisen as to the feasibility of a course of action. This is *not* to be construed as a lack of trust and confidence on the part of the manager; it is simply evidence of the fact that he takes his job seriously and is not about to make any errors of omission in carrying out his responsibilities.

As indicated a few pages back, the monitoring function of the manager can give rise to some deep problems unless he is exceptionally perceptive in dealing with others. Basically, the monitoring activity is a negative one; it usually results in something *not* happening, or in someone *not* being allowed to do something. At least two attributes should be actively cultivated by the manager here. On the one hand, he must go to whatever lengths are necessary to be sure that he has tight emotional control over himself. Things will get abrasive enough without his contributing to the upset by losing his temper or by making unfortunate remarks to others.

On the other hand, the manager must take whatever steps are necessary to be sure that his people know he will be fair and honest in his dealings with them. They are human, and they might be forgiven for feeling at times that the boss is manipulating them or is being less than fair with them when he denies them things they want, especially if they are convinced that this is the proper way to go.

The trouble is, the manager will have to make these value judgments about censorship without a great deal of data to support his thinking. Many times it will be purely intuitive and the subordinate probably will know that this is the case. When this happens, there most certainly will be headbutting, and the manager will have to prove his objectivity and his lack of bias. Only when this has been done can he hope to maintain a viable working relationship with subordinates. The importance of this cannot be missed by anyone.

In "playing God," which is what he is doing in the monitoring process, the manager will find more occasions to mistrust his own judgments than in any other area of his work. The attitude of the subordinate involved will have its effect in the long run. The employee will be asking both himself and his manager why he is not being allowed to pursue a certain course of action. And if, as previously indicated, the manager has been forced to make an intuitive value judgment, largely unsupported by facts, he will naturally be upset and wonder whether his judgment was a good one.

In the long run, there is little help or comfort for the manager in his monitoring role except to practice it as the occasion demands and to learn from the events which occur during this learning process. Here is another area of management where nothing can take the place of years of experience, *if proper learning has resulted from that experience.* All managers have about the same kind of experience in their backgrounds; it is the ones who can learn from the past who will win.

We should be remiss not to note that the managerial activity of monitoring will be strongly influenced by the managerial style adopted by the leader. The heavy taskmaster will be inclined to monitor much more closely than the permissive type of leader. Which of the two will have the better results is decided by many converging variables, but one of the strongest of them is the matter of leadership style.

ACTING AGAINST DYSFUNCTIONAL ACTIVITIES

Once the manager has made a value judgment that a course of action or an activity is dysfunctional, his path is clear before him: Action must be taken at once to change whatever is being done wrong or to implement that which is not being done. For the morale of the group, for the good of the organization, and for the future of the manager, this action must be taken as soon as the judgment has been made. This does not mean that the manager will overreact and do something impulsive, without proper planning. But it must not seem to his observers that he is indecisive or hesitant to make a move where it is indicated. This matter of appearance is of utmost importance to the manager, because it has such a great influence on his reputation and that of his group.

As we have just seen, this is a situation where the manager will not have a long time in which to do his planning. He will be pressured by the necessity of moving fast and decisively, so his procedure for and choice of alternative routes must be done in a very short time. In looking for corrective action, the leader must be certain that he has made a correct diagnosis of what went wrong before. It is not enough simply to condemn a method of operation until he has cited the fundamental reasons for the misfiring of the operation. Then, naturally, the planning will involve how to remove these elements and what to substitute for them.

This is one of the lonelier situations of managerial life. The leader cannot in all honesty involve his subordinates very deeply in this planning action, since it is a high-risk situation and is essentially the leader's responsibility rather than that of his subordinates. Certainly it is acceptable to check individual parts of the decision with any member of the group who might have greater expertise than does the manager, but in the last analysis this is a decision the manager must make on his own.

At the same time, this situation demands the best kind of managerial communication with subordinates. The leader must be sure that all his followers know exactly what went wrong and why. (Incidentally, this is another case where we are much more concerned with *what* was wrong than with *who* was wrong.) They must be convinced that the group was on the wrong trail before they will be willing to take another one. Obviously, the leader must also communicate his new plans, and do it in such a manner that he gains reasonable acceptance for the new course of action before it is initiated. We have enough resistance to change as it is without running the risk of intensifying it.

It is entirely possible that the change or changes decided upon by the manager will require some major reshuffling of his organization. Perhaps some of the bad elements of the old way of doing things were associated with misplacement of people or less than proper usage of their expertise and abilities. In some cases there may be really significant changes, perhaps even involving some inversions of hierarchical positions. Personal and interpersonal upsets of this kind are only natural in a yeasty and changing organizational scene. We shall explore more fully the maintenance of interpersonal relationships in the censorship function later in the chapter.

When the planning has been done, the proper alternative chosen, and the necessary organizational alterations decided upon and communicated, the manager should proceed immediately with complete implementation of the change. The sooner it is done, the quicker employees will recover from the dysfunctional actions which had been taking place and the quicker there will be observable improvement in the work of the group. This, after all, is what the manager wants and works for all the time.

During the entire process the manager will be smart to keep upper echelons completely informed of what is going on and what changes are being contemplated. They will be concerned about and interested in several things: his diagnosis of the problem, his appraisal of what things should be changed, the methodology he proposes to change things around, and his handling of his people during what is probably a time of crisis. In other words, his entire performance as a manager will be under review by *his* managers while he is performing this part of the censorship function.

The manager's coordinating of this series of events will not be totally complete until he has tied in other groups and peers who will be affected by the upcoming changes. In many cases these people will make or break the proposed action, and it is certainly to the manager's distinct advantage to have them understand thoroughly what he is proposing and to have their agreement to whatever changes they will be faced with because of his decisions. This is a time when the manager needs them — badly.

It is quite obvious that the manager has not finished his job simply by implementing a new procedure or methodology in place of one that was dysfunctional. It will be his responsibility as group leader to monitor the new scene closely until he is sure that the results achieved are what he had hoped for. Follow-up and evaluation are mandatory here, so that if it is necessary to abandon this method and choose another alternative the manager can do it the moment he has decided the original change was a mistake. Since he has already alerted his bosses to what he has been doing, they will be following his results closely and with interest. The manager should try to avoid having them come forth with negative responses to his decisions and actions; he should beat them to the punch if further changes seem to be indicated as a result of the first action.

MAINTAINING INTERPERSONAL RELATIONSHIPS

As we have already seen, it is nearly impossible for the manager to inaugurate major changes in the operation of his department without having some abrasions occur in the complex interpersonal relationships within his group. The very process of censorship is bound to upset some or many of the people involved, since they are going to have to change their method of operation significantly. How, then, is the manager to go about repairing these damaged interfaces within his group?

The first and most obvious general method for keeping upsets at a minimum, or repairing them if they occur, is for the manager to demonstrate by attitudes and actions that he is being as objective about the whole matter as is humanly possible. If he can demonstrate irrefutably that he is concerned with the process of the group and that nobody is considered "to blame" for any activities which have to be changed, the manager is nearly home free. Although it is impossible under these conditions to give great thought to the feelings of the employees who have to modify their behavior, it is still true that they will react less negatively if they can see beyond doubt that the manager is making these changes not on the basis of personalities but rather on the facts as they present themselves to his analysis. If the employees affected have any modicum of fairness in them, they will see that whatever effects have an impact on them personally do *not* come from any personal design by their leader.

Next, it is incumbent upon the leader to plan carefully for the organizational changes which may have to be accomplished as a result of censorship activities within the operations under his charge. By proper placement of teams and subgroups, it is often possible to avoid direct confrontation between those who have had their situations changed. The leader should be aware of likes and dislikes of those working for him, and it may be possible to structure subgroups in such a way that these conflict situations are held to a minimum. In any event, this should be looked at quite carefully by the manager before he makes reassignments which will materially affect the personnel of small work units. This kind of thinking cannot hurt and will many times be of material advantage to the entire work group.

Third, there are situations, unavoidable under any circumstances, when it will be necessary to force a direct confrontation between individuals in order to accomplish the desired objectives. In this action, which will come as a last resort on the part of the manager, the best approach is to stage and referee the meetings between the people involved. By recognizing the difficulties, facing them, and working them out on a cooperative basis, the manager can often avoid engendering enduring enmities among those who feel that their position in the group has deteriorated or who perhaps feel that they have been mistreated. Once again, the important thing is for the manager to recognize the need for an objective approach and to demonstrate it during the confrontation and discussion of the interpersonal problems.

Fourth, occasionally there will be a hangover of bad feelings between two or more employees, or between a group of employees and the manager. The manager will then have to continue to work at resolving the difficulties and mending the fences in the personal interfaces which have been damaged. Here the keyword is patience. Human nature is such that many times the first effort is not enough, but repeated returns to a discussion of the problem will eventually do the job of improving relationships. These times are real challenges to the leadership of the manager and in the main furnish a chance for the true practice of management. A victory in one of these is a citation to the professionalism of the manager involved.

Finally, the manager must always remember that he can't win them all. Once in a while there will be an upset between two or more people that is irreparable and that no amount of time or effort can restore. If the manager comes to this considered decision after he has spent a reasonable amount of time and effort at shoring things up, then his duty once more is clear and definitive. Since the manager's final responsibility is always "the best for the most," he may have to remove one or more of the dissidents from the group so that the rest of the people can exist in harmony. The one thing that cannot be allowed to happen is to have ongoing personal differences interfere with getting the job done. If this seems imminent, some transfers or terminations may be mandatory.

In this chapter we have been looking at one of the more difficult (and sometimes less pleasant) aspects of the managerial job. The manager is saddled with the responsibility of censoring the activities of the work force; this is crystal clear and undeniable. This monitoring process is continuing and continuous. The manager should make of it a conditioned reflex so that he can monitor and censor his group's activities without having to consciously remind himself of its necessity.

The censorship function requires many, many value judgments from the manager, and these must often be made quickly, with perhaps fewer data than the manager would prefer. But made they must be. Then, if a method or an activity is judged to be dysfunctional, the manager at once must find a substitute methodology which has a reasonable chance of repairing the problem and proceed forthwith to implement it in place of what was wrong before. Finally, the manager must watch carefully over the interpersonal relationships of the group throughout these changes to keep them as viable as possible under the circumstances.

It is in the continuation of the monitoring function that managers grow and develop in their work. It is a great separator of the mature from the immature manager.

6

THE MANAGER
AS A
PARENT FIGURE

Every employee in an organization either consciously or unconsciously looks to his supervisor as a parent figure. This is irrespective of their comparative chronological ages and is a product of the employee's conditioning in the family situation as he was growing up. It is another of the factors which complicate the managerial job, and the supervisor will have to vary his own behavior in order to accommodate this vector.

THIS RESPONSIBILITY IS A MUST

Many managers, especially the younger ones, shy away from this responsibility and find it exceedingly difficult to accept as an ongoing part of their job. There are several reasons why the group leader *must* take on this segment of the job or fail in complete fulfillment of what is expected of him.

First, as we have already seen, his subordinates will expect it of him. The leader is there; he has been designated as a leader; he must lead or his followers will be confused, feel rejected, and eventually dissociate from the organization. The situation is analogous to that of the family itself. If a child feels that either parent is not accepting him, his trauma will increase until it becomes insupportable, and his behavior will become increasingly dysfunctional to the point of being completely and irrevocably deviant.

In the working situation the new employee has a right to expect a welcome from his supervisor and to have continuing support from his leader, not only during the indoctrination period but for the duration of the working relationship. Just as the child looks to his parents for a greater knowledge and wisdom in the ways of life, so the employee expects his supervisor to have the great majority of the answers to the questions which will naturally arise. This is not to say that the boss must be omniscient, but if he doesn't have the answer it is his duty to make an effort to find it.

Second, it is greatly to the advantage of the supervisor to assume this duty. If this is done, the relationship he builds with a subordinate will be much deeper, more lasting, and more productive for both of them. One of the principal reasons for the continued growth and prosperity of labor unions, long after their original cause for being has disappeared, is that management in general throughout the country has been derelict in its duty of making the employee feel needed and wanted, while the unions have worked assiduously at that effort. If the employee cannot find evidence that his nominal leadership has an interest in him personally, he will turn to the other source at hand, which does display a need and a want for his membership and association.

In a more positive framework, the manager will be more popular, more effective, and probably much more promotable as a result of these strong, well-founded relationships with his people. He will soon discover that when the necessity arises he can go to his people and ask the extra effort with a reasonable chance of its being given, just as most children will respond favorably to a call for assistance from their parents.

Third, the manager's superiors will in most cases expect this from him and will mark him down in overall performance if they see evidence that he is shirking this part of his job duties. There may be no overt verbalization from superiors in this area, since it is a sensitive one, but failure to act in this will weaken the overall appraisal of his work as a leader. As noted earlier, many managers are reticent — even embarrassed — to play the parent role; if they hear nothing specific about it from their managers, they may mistakenly think that nothing has been noticed about their lack.

It is perfectly true that human beings have a wide variety of ability to both feel and express a parent-sibling relationship, but this will be understood by our subordinates. The requisite is that there be some indication of recognition on the part of the manager that this is an integral part of his job.

On the plus side, when this relationship has been established and reinforced, it is much easier for the manager to enforce whatever discipline may be necessary through the course of employment. The employee has been conditioned to expect discipline from his parents; if the relationship on the job with the boss is a similar one, discipline will be an expectation, not a purely punitive measure taken by a hostile and cold-blooded superior.

At the same time, it will obviously be much easier and more natural to give positive reinforcement to good performance if this general sort of climate has been established. If the subordinate truly can look at his leader *in loco parentis,* nothing could be more right than for the parent figure to show appreciation for good behavior as well as to chastise bad actions. On the other hand, if no attempt has ever been made to develop these feelings, it will be awkward, embarrassing, and artificial to have the supervisor come forth with "appreciation" of good work.

In general, we can only reiterate that the parent role is a basic managerial responsibility which cannot be avoided but which, on the contrary, must be worked at carefully and continually. Naturally, since there is no real kinship present, there are times when personal bias will intrude and make it more difficult to assume and carry on this posture; but this fact does nothing to alter the fundamental necessity for making the effort. Once arrived at on the part of all involved, the familial type of organization will have much more flexibility and latitude of action than an organization set up on more formal and rigid bases.

EXPLAINING MANAGERIAL ACTIONS

As decisions are passed from level to level within a hierarchy, there are many chances for poor communication and misunderstandings to happen. It is certainly no wonder that employees are sometimes confused and disturbed by what they read as coming from executives of the enterprise. Moreover, it is entirely to be expected that they will turn to their supervisor for "the word" about what is going on, just as children turn to their parents for explanations about a strange world. The manager must stand ready to take on this chore whenever his people come to him with questions.

The easiest case, of course, is when there is a simple misunderstanding of what is meant by a new policy or procedure. Here the supervisor can clear the air just by telling his subordinate what the real intent is and explaining how it will change the procedure. Every time he takes this action, the leader is further cementing the structure of a viable relationship between him and his people; every time he fails to do it, he is running the risk of damaging his relationships with his people, perhaps irreparably.

The situation is much cloudier in those cases in which the manager himself is not entirely sold on the new policy. Even if he has been offered an opportunity to make his inputs before the decision was made, the decision may go against his thinking and beliefs, and then he is in trouble in trying to explain the new situation to his people. If he has been unable to buy the rationale by which the executive echelon has propounded the policy, it will be nearly impossible to sell it to his people. Even if they buy it themselves, it is all too likely that they will see his hesitancy and lack of belief in what will be done. Obviously, there is but one course for the manager to take: He *must* continue to implement the change with all his energies and make certain that his people conform to the new norms, whatever he may think about them personally. He too must conform.

Another situation which will require explanation from the group leader is when conflict develops between two different managers and their respective crews. In this case it is entirely probable that the actions of the manager will condition the response and the thinking of his people — in other words, he will determine where their sympathies lie and which side they will try to help in the conflict. It is not germane for the leader to draw back and give forth preachments about how wrong it is to get into a battle with another group; since work crews are made up of human beings, it is inevitable that this will happen with considerable frequency. The greater responsibility of the group leader demands that he follow the twists and turns of the conflict with extreme accuracy, because the situation can change to such an extent that he and his people will find it necessary either to change sides suddenly or perhaps to extricate themselves completely from the interchange and become neutral.

The manager's responsibility to his people goes far beyond the simple interpretation of what is already going on. He must also interpret to his people the long-range plans of the enterprise, to the best of his knowledge of them. With the scene changing so rapidly today, every person has a right to as much knowledge as is available about what is coming up around the corner, to be readied for delivery one, two, or five years from now. The longer the leadtime the manager can give his people for changes to come, the better they can prepare themselves mentally and the easier their adjustment will be to the new face of the work situation.

It is entirely possible that changes in the work situation will require retraining or further education for workers, and it is eminently unfair if this is sprung on them with no previous preparation. Incidentally, we are entering an era where continuing education will be an absolute must for everyone who wants to remain competitive in business, or even to save the job he or she now holds. We can no longer be trained for any job and expect that this will be it; things transmute too rapidly, and our technology is exploding too fast for this to happen again.

We can reinforce the necessity for communication between the manager and his people by reminding ourselves that up to a very few years ago the great majority of managers operated under the belief that the less workers knew of what was going on, the better it was for all concerned. Naturally, this is in complete negation of fundamental principles of human psychology, since all of us want to know why we are required to do those things we must on the job.

Lastly, the manager must most certainly explain to his people his own actions. It is easy to fall into the trap of believing that our people understand what we are doing "because we know each other so well." This can be a far cry from the real truth, and the manager who fails to keep his people informed of the reasons for his actions is playing Russian roulette with his interpersonal relationships and his entire career. If anything, his people have a greater stake in his actions than in those of any other manager in the organization, because what he does will affect them more quickly and vitally than it will anyone else.

It is interesting how often we come back to the term "communication" in discussing the job of the manager. We all know, intellectually, that talking with others is a large part of our job, but we sometimes fail to remember the complete and overriding importance of good communication in every facet of the managerial job.

INVOLVEMENT IN PERSONAL PROBLEMS

One of the more troublesome jobs for any manager is to decide how far to involve himself in the personal problems of a subordinate. If the relationship between them is good, and the employee comes naturally and regularly to the boss with job-related problems, it is difficult to turn him away when he seeks advice on personal problems without endangering the closeness which it has taken years to build. Yet the manager is aware that if his advice and counsel cause the subordinate to do something which he regrets later, he will almost certainly blame the supervisor for his actions and turn against him.

An even more cogent reason for not getting too deeply

involved in personal problems is that many times they concern emotional or mental difficulties which the manager is eminently unqualified to handle. There is terrific temptation for the leader to try to be a therapist, especially when he knows his employee intimately and can usually predict his behavior well. To succumb to this pull and try to give professional counsel to the employee will almost certainly end in disaster, for as we all know only a minute percentage of managers are trained as psychotherapists or psychiatrists.

The managerial function here is to act as a catalyst and to help the employee get qualified professional help. This much is our duty; anything beyond this point where emotional upsets are part of the picture is an invasion of the employee's privacy and cannot be condoned on the part of the manager. We must remember that in the family situation, too, parents will not go very far in trying to treat emotional or mental illness in their children but will seek medical or psychological advice. The same thing should occur in the business scene, where the manager represents a parent figure to all his employees.

Personal problems which involve other members of the employee's family should be approached with the same kind of care. Although it is foolish to tell our employees they must leave their personal problems at home, since they can't any more than we can, their involvement with and love for their families will soon get them as much in the act as if the problem were their own. Actually, there may be more danger for the boss if he gets involved here, because the problem is one step removed from the employee, and the manager will not have established a relationship with the family members who are in trouble.

If there is any one methodology which may be used from time to time with discretion in these scenes, it is nondirective counseling. The manager who has learned to listen creatively has a great tool for helping any employee. Many times all that the employee needs to get himself started is to have someone to whom he can talk freely and openly, someone who he knows will respect his confidences completely and absolutely. Simply by talking with someone who is interested and friendly, the troubled employee can often start to work his way through his problem and may succeed in solving it completely, with no help from anyone except the boss, who has functioned solely as a listening post. However, nondirective counseling is not often an innate ability; the tendency to give advice in these circumstances is a strong one, and the manager will have to exert much will power to keep his activity in the nondirective boundary. But, to reinforce, if this can be learned, it can be invaluable to the supervisor in working with employees who have personal problems.

In other sorts of personal problems the indicated action may be entirely different. If an employee has gotten himself into financial trouble, the boss may be in a particularly good position to give sound advice. He may also be able to arrange meetings with creditors so that they can know the manager is aware of the trouble and is actively engaged in trying to reduce the problem. More than that, it might be possible for the leader to see that the financially burdened employee get some temporary overtime so that the extra income can be applied to the pressing debts.

Many companies still have stringent policies about garnishments against employees; some even fire an employee for two or more garnishments within a short period. This sort of company policy has traces of medieval debtors' prisoner in it, but if the policy is there, the manager can sometimes work around it to the advantage of the employee. Once again, if the creditor knows that the boss is trying to help the employee, there may be much less chance for a garnishment being filed. Possibly salary assignments can be worked out amicably while heavy indebtedness is being reduced over a time period.

We can generalize by saying that the manager's involvement in the personal problems of an employee will be a function of his knowledge of himself, the employee, and his experience in the ways they have interacted before. Essentially, this means that every employee will be approached differently, and that the supervisor might get seriously involved in the personal problems of one subordinate while staying almost completely clear of those of another employee.

Another decision usually associated with involvement with an employee's problem is how much to communicate of it and to whom. The manager may have been completely sincere at first in promising that he will keep inviolate all confidences, only to become extremely troubled later when he realizes that others must be called into the action if there is to be a viable solution. At this point, of course, he must go back to the employee and get his permission to talk with someone else. If permission is not forthcoming, the employer should withdraw from any further activity in connection with his employee's personal problem.

THE MANAGER AS A TRAINER

As a manager and supervisor, the group leader spends more time teaching than in any other single activity. The new employee must be trained and checked; the older employee must be informed about changes in process or procedures so as not to become obsolescent in the working sphere.

At this point we must make a strong pitch for the supervisor/manager *not* to delegate the matter of training if it is at all possible to keep it a personal part of the job. In the first place, it is extremely hard to find a nonmanagement person who has the same commitment to the job and to the enterprise as does a manager. Even though the nonmanager may be a good teacher and may enjoy training, it is unlikely that he will be as involved in the process, or as exacting in the end result, as would the manager if he were doing the training. If the supervisor is at all concerned about the quality of performance which will come out of the training, he should do it.

Second, there is no other way of getting so close so quickly to the new employee as to be his mentor at the entering step. He will automatically look to his trainer for the answers to all his problems on the job, and if this is not the group leader, there will not be the same desirable relationship between them as would result from the supervisor doing the training.

Third, by training the employee himself, the manager can avoid some of the problems arising with the union representative. When a new employee does not have a close relationship with his superior, he will naturally turn to another who does express a close personal interest in him—and that, we can be sure, will most often be a union representative.

Nothing in this should be construed to mean that I am anti-union; on the contrary, most of my industrial life was spent working with several of the major American unions from the management side. But I do think it deplorable when management abdicates and allows the union to take over both its spot and that which naturally should be occupied by the supervisor of the group. Both sides must participate in the development of employees if we are to have normal and viable working relationships on the job. This is one of our major objectives.

As our technology becomes increasingly complex, we are finding work groups where several disciplines are mixed together and where it is impossible for the manager to have enough expertise in all of them to do the actual training. In these situations the supervisor's job becomes more difficult, but it is far from hopeless. Perhaps the manager was trained as a mechanical engineer and now finds himself supervising mechanical, electrical, and chemical engineers. The manager will still have enough general skill in engineering to be able to tell when the work done in other disciplines is satisfactory and when it is not. In all probability he would not be able to tell exactly what was wrong in another area, but he would know that the desired results were not being achieved and would be able to tell who was failing in his assignment.

It is obvious in this situation that the training of an entering employee whose expertise lies in other fields will have to be delegated, but overall responsibility and accountability for the new employee is never lost by the direct supervisor. Here his training activity will be centered in *choosing and training a trainer.* It is an interesting fact that the most brilliant performer in a given field is often *not* the best teacher or trainer of that subject. This can arise because the bright performer fails to recognize the traps and pitfalls in the field for the less brilliant student. He may have difficulty relating to the problems of the average performer and thereby fail to make the points necessary to overcome these rough spots.

The manager will often do better to reject the intellectual or "bookish" performer in a given area and look instead for a person who likes to teach and who has a real desire to help other people learn their jobs properly and well. This chosen trainer should then be given formal instruction in how to teach and be put into situations as often as possible where he can practice the training activity. One thing is mandatory: The supervisor has the responsibility for checking both the trainer and the trainee frequently during the training process. Results can never be assumed; they must be followed up repeatedly until the manager has satisfied himself that the newcomer is comfortably and productively settled into the job.

The manager's training responsibilities are not restricted to those who are working *for* him. In some aspects of the job the manager must stand ready to train his boss as well. This is especially true when changes occur within the work group that higher-ups would not know about unless they were directly informed. This kind of communication should be undertaken by the manager of the group, and he should reassure himself that the loop is closed by checking his boss's understanding of what is going on. It is also the manager's duty to communicate with his peers in other departments, especially if their activities interlock with his department or if changes are being inaugurated which will have an impact on the other groups. The manager is responsible for getting the new information to all who have a right to know what is going on.

As previously stated, the amount of managerial time consumed by the training process is the largest single part of the supervisor's job. Enormous amounts of effort will be spent in doing this over the lifetime of the manager's career.

THE SUPPORTIVE CLIMATE

There is, of course, a broad spectrum of parental attitudes toward the young. But by far the majority of parents feel protective toward their children and make every effort to support them in their good activities and to correct them when they are wrong. The smart manager will also try to be supportive toward his employees whenever possible, because of the easily demonstrable better results obtained when the leader maintains this posture. Most people respond favorably toward a friendly approach from their leader and will be more inclined to give forth extra effort if the leader has indicated by his manner that he expects his people to be good.

This concept in no way indicates that the leader will coddle his people or be overprotective of them when they have problems. What it does mean is that supervisors and managers will always be there as resource people when the going gets tough for the workers and will stand ready to give assistance when the need is indicated. If the employee has been properly oriented and trained in his job, these situations will be minimized, but it is inevitable that from time to time problems will arise which should evoke support from the manager. We shall have more to say about this later.

One of the areas where it is especially important for the manager to be supportive is in the self-development of the subordinate. We all have great difficulty in being truly objective about ourselves, and the manager should remember this when talking or working with subordinates. With his broader and deeper backlog of experience, the supervisor should in almost all cases be able to give cogent suggestions to his people about promising tools and activities which will result in their positive development on the job.

It is most crucial that the manager remain supportive when an employee has been in error or is subjected to criticism by others. This does not mean that he should defend the *action*, but he must defend the *person* from degradation of his position or permanent loss of self-esteem. It is in times of travail that the manager's leadership should be most strongly and positively exhibited. Then, when he is sure that no damage has been done to the individual, the leader can step in and make of the mistake a learning experience for improved performance and better understanding downstream. This should be the job of the modern industrial leader.

At the same time, the manager must remember that he has a larger and broader responsibility: *He must be supportive of the entire group as well.* It is sometimes very difficult to balance his duty to the individual and his duty to the group to the improvement of both and the harm of neither. If an employee has made a mistake which resulted in harm to the entire group, he will probably be up for punishment from his peers. It is at this point that the leader must exhibit his most delicate leadership. Actually, his position here becomes one of mediator and feather smoother. He should explain to the group how such a mistake could happen honestly and with no malice intended, at the same time demonstrating to the errant employee how his action resulted in harm to the group and why he should change his methods in the future.

We have talked before of how hard it is to determine to what extent a manager should implicate himself in the personal problems of his employees and of the wide variations this depth of involvement will evince. One thing, however, is certain. The manager must always be as supportive as possible whenever one of his subordinates is under personal stress and trauma. It is at these times that the leader will strongly emerge as a parent figure in the thinking of the troubled employee; if the leader is clearly there as a rock in the wilderness, the relationship between the two will be solidly cemented for all future time of their association. The supervisor may be able to do nothing whatever about the problem itself, but he must demonstrate that he is unwaveringly behind his subordinate as a person.

It should be clear that such an attribute on the part of the group leader will have a serendipitous effect for him. When the time comes that he is in trouble, his people will support him just as solidly as he supported them when they had problems. He can then cash many IOUs he wasn't even aware were being banked for him because of his previous actions.

To reinforce, the assumption of a conscious role as a parent figure is one of the harder tasks a manager faces. Yet it is becoming increasingly important in his total job, as a result of the burgeoning complexity of business and social living in this civilization. Moreover, this aspect of the manager's job is seldom mentioned by his superiors when they are inducting him into management. This must be changed. The new manager can be saved much personal embarrassment and upset if it is clearly indicated that this quasiparental position is a natural part of his job. Even if there are some inversions of chronological age between the manager and his people, he will still be expected to assume this role and maintain it unfalteringly.

This concept must be integrated into the individual's managerial philosophy early in his or her training, because it affects so many other segments of the total position. What we are really saying is that nobody can become a well-rounded, total manager until this has been thought through and the proper action taken.

7

THE MANAGER AND SOCIAL RESPONSIBILITY

One of the more heartening aspects of the managerial scene is the significant change which has occurred within the past twenty or twenty-five years in the thinking of executives and managers regarding social responsibility. Before that time, the average American manager would have scorned and ridiculed any statement that business and industry had any real social duty to the general public. He might even have been embarrassed in considering the idea. This is no longer so. There is a wide variation along the spectrum of social duty, but almost every manager today will admit, if pressed, that there is some.

THE CHANGING SCENE IN AMERICAN BUSINESS

How has this thinking manifested itself in America? First of all, there has been a spate of legislation within the past few years dealing with the impact of business and industry on the American society. Most of this legislation is concerned with the ecosystem of the country. It is true that some of it has levied immense costs on industry in order to conform. The important thing is that, with few exceptions, industry has made little concerted effort to evade these actions totally. In some cases negotiations were carried on to reduce the total dollar effect of the legislation on individual business, but there was either tacit or overt acceptance of the general responsibility by almost all the major industries affected.

For example, the general management population quickly accepted the implications of the Occupational Safety and Health Act. As originally stated, this legislation might have been considered the death warrant for most medium- and small-sized American business; but after a frightened stirring for the first few months, the reaction on the part of the businessman was to settle down to find ways and means to comply with the myriad of regulations generated by the federal government in this area. Fortunately, up to this time at least, the government has maintained a fairly reasonable attitude toward the entire matter and has not insisted on compliance to the actual wording of all the regulations generated. Had the government done so, a large percentage of American businesses would have been bankrupted.

Second, it is interesting to note how many annual reports and advertisements deal with questions of corporate social responsibility, especially matters of an ecological nature already mentioned. The commercials for Exxon in their weekend national news broadcasts are nearly always in an ecological vein. The posture seems sometimes defensive, but the acknowledgment of duties is there.

Third, there has been widespread recognition, both publicly and privately, by our managerial population of social duties to the individual employee of the firm. Actually, the vast increases in fringe benefits have *not* all been forced on management; many of them have originated there, rather than with employees. We continually see increased coverage in sick leave, vacations, retirement benefits, and programs for the rehabilitation of alcoholics and drug addicts. Programs for the training of elderly employees for retirement are multiplying across the country, engendered by management's awareness that retirement can be traumatic — even fatal — to the employee who has not been properly prepared for the changes involved in this momentous step.

An interesting case in point is the rapid proliferation of company-subsidized adult-education programs for employees.

The significant trend here is that companies no longer make a strict demand that such education be job-related. Top management in many concerns is coming to realize that personal growth and self-development are important per se for the mental health of the employee, whether or not he uses the subject matter directly on the job.

Of special significance is the fact that many companies are now beginning to *initiate* programs in recognition of social responsibility on their own volition, rather than waiting to be pressured into them by aroused employees. This can only have a salutary effect on the overall employee relations picture and will redound to the benefit of everyone.

It is important that a point be made here for clarification. An admission and realization of social responsibility on the part of management does not necessarily mean that managers have "gone soft" or will coddle their employees. In fact, the tough-minded manager may actually have a fuller realization of his social responsibility than does a weak or vacillating manager. The willful manager will know more certainly that a realistic and viable relationship must be built between management and labor if the organization's objectives are to be reached fully. He also knows that employees have a more penetrating awareness of what is coming to them from the company and that they will not be put off long by vague, unkept promises. The realistic manager knows that his people must have faces for him, and that he must be cognizant of their individual differences in their needs and expectations from the job.

WHAT DO WE OWE OUR PEOPLE?

The question of the social responsibility of managers toward the people who work for them will be answered differently by almost every manager. The concept is conditioned both by the managerial philosophy of the company and by the individual thinking of the manager. Perhaps, however, we can state some general principles which would be accepted by the majority of managers. First, and of overriding importance, we do owe employees something for the fact that they are entrusting themselves and their futures to our organization and to our leadership. Of all the places they might have gone to look for work, they have chosen ours, and have said, in effect, that they judge us worthy of this heavy responsibility. This choice on the part of the working person is one of the most important decisions of a lifetime—second only to the choice of a mate.

For this reason, it is obvious and above argument that we owe employees a decent living wage and that we must monitor the level of their pay continuously to see that it is kept reasonably in line. Pay has many more implications than its simple buying power. Closely associated with the amount of our wages is the status, the feeling of personal achievement, and the ego satisfaction we feel from being well paid.

Next, we owe it to our employees to offer to the public a product or a service which is socially useful. Any organization which does not do so is a social parasite and should be done away with. This still leaves an almost infinitely wide spectrum of goods and services from which to choose as the basis for founding a commercial firm. It is all too true, unfortunately, that there are many money-making firms which do not lie within this category. As managers, we have an individual responsibility to steer clear of this kind of employment, both for ourselves and for those who work for us.

One of the first social duties of the employer to be the object of public concern was the matter of working conditions, and this is still one of the larger areas of confrontation and dispute. No employer who subjects his people to health hazards on the job should be allowed to continue operations. Any demonstrable hazard must be corrected immediately before the employer is given license to continue. We have already mentioned the stir which OSHA caused after its enactment, but there can be no question of the validity of its overall purpose: the protection of the health of all industrial and business employees at whatever level.

In the matter of general social duty, a strong argument could be made that any employer owes his people an opportunity to better themselves on the job whenever they are ready for it.

If the desire for advancement is present, the worker should be given a chance to realize this wish. This naturally presents some rather extreme problems in some businesses, but we now have a tool which is exceedingly useful in this area: job enrichment. If there is blockage in the vertical ascent in the hierarchy, allowing the person to grow and develop *within the same job* will many times satisfy his needs. The essential thing is that the employee not see himself as trapped within a tight, constricting job. When this happens, he will lose all motivation, and the quality of his work will inevitably suffer.

We owe our people honesty and candor in all our dealings, both on and off the job. A tight compartmentalization of our lives into segments of "on the job" and "off the job" is no longer possible. What we do at work and what we do at home are intermeshed, no matter how hard we may try to separate them in our thinking. Therefore, the manager is under the obligation of being sure that his people have the complete and true word about what is going on as nearly as he knows it himself. If this one concept alone were truly implemented by all managers, a vast majority of problems in connection with work and working people would disappear.

Maintaining secrecy where it is not needed is the single most prevalent managerial crime. We rationalize it by saying "It's for the good of the employee," often when we don't even believe this ourselves, and deep down we know that many secrets are kept from our workers just to bolster our feelings of managerial power and position. This is never defensible and can only result in bad sentiments and ruptures in the relationships between workers and their managers.

There is one social duty of the employer which is still widely debated and treated very differently in different organizations. This is the question of the company's responsibility to long-service employees. How far should the employer go in protecting the job of a man or woman who has served well and faithfully for, say, twenty years, and then becomes unable to perform for reasons of bad health or technical obsolescence? As stated, there are wide variations here. Some companies will cut the superannuated employee off without a moment's hesitation, while others will go to great lengths to see that the employee has some kind of job left with the company as repayment for many years of service.

It will never be possible to settle this question to the complete satisfaction of all managers. But it is abundantly obvious that there is a growing trend toward the recognition of some kind of duty inherent in the accumulation of a long period of good service. Many of the large unions have already made this a matter of negotiation in an effort to secure some kind of protection for the older or sick employee. To say that such things are categorically impossible is to fly in the face of the truth: Japan became a world industrial power while perpetuating its "strange" custom of giving lifetime employment to all workers. If the Japanese could do it, so can we!

WHAT DO WE OWE THE ENTERPRISE?

Before we get too engrossed in our duties to our employees, we should stop to consider what our debts are to our employers. As managers, we have a greater involvement with and responsibility to the enterprise than do the people who work for us. This is a part of the obligation we take on when we become managers, and it will be with us as long as we remain in our jobs.

First of all, no matter how it may bother us at times, we are more than eight-hour employees. Our doctors, our spouses, and our families will all remind us, with a certain amount of acerbity from time to time, that we do have duties other than to our employers, and they are right. Nevertheless, in order to do our jobs well and effectively, we will many times find our workday extending significantly beyond the stated hours of nine to five, or whatever. This is completely logical and natural when we stop to consider that we are coordinating and planning the work for several other people. These activities will be governed by what is going on currently on the job: the status of production, the quality of work, and the imminence of deadlines.

This means that the average manager will discover his workload to follow a curve roughly sinusoidal in nature, with recurrent high and low spots in the flow of activities. There is little that can be done to anticipate these differences in pressures, so it is hardly ever possible to plan for and smooth out these changes in tempo. The manager simply has to be braced for such times and learn to live with them.

From the standpoint of social betterment, managers have another responsibility to their employers not always considered and planned for in their work. This is our duty to give inputs to management above us whenever we observe things that will affect the company's impact on the public. In the kaleidoscopic mix we live in today it is possible for a large firm to begin to have an effect on the social climate of its community without even being aware of it at first. The manager who spots this effect owes it to his company to communicate his observations upstairs. Moreover, if his words do not elicit any action, the manager must be ready to go back as many times as necessary to get something started.

The manager has more than a personal stake in his growth and development and those of his people. It is his clear-cut duty to engage in these activities as a method of fulfilling his obligation to the firm. In order for his employers to remain competitive down the road, they are going to have to change and adapt, just as any other individual or business enterprise must do in life's complex interactions. It will be much better and more economical for the company to put some time, effort, and money into bringing along its own employees, rather than to discard them as they become obsolescent and then have to make tremendous investments in new employees. The comparative economics of this are indisputable. The individual manager has an unremitting obligation to the company with respect to the development of those for whom he is responsible.

Along with the duties to the company already mentioned, the manager should charge himself with scanning the scene outside the company's action arena for trends which might have an effect internally. Many, many subcultures are formed within our society over the years. How many of them appear likely to persist or even grow larger? If they do, what probable effect will they have on the company? What should the actions of the company be to adjust to this foreseen impact? Or, on the other hand, should anything out of the ordinary be done? These decisions will not often be made by any single manager, but his duty in reporting what he believes to be social trends on the outside is clear and ongoing.

It is, of course, dangerous to generalize on the matter of the manager's individual duty to the enterprise, since there is such a wide variation in company philosophies and methods of operations, just as there are tremendous differences among managers themselves. What is viable and comfortable for a given manager in one company may be completely untenable for that manager in another company. It is up to the manager to seek out the guidelines by which he can accommodate himself to his own philosophy and that of his company, since many of the decisions to be made in this area will be his and his alone. (We are speaking here of the methods which will be necessary to make the required adjustments.)

One observation might be helpful in our thinking along these lines. All of this discussion on the manager's social responsibility is totally irrelevant in the case of the Theory X manager. He is not mentally geared to consider the social impact of his managerial actions; to him they are not worth thinking about. Essentially, we are saying that our entire management population will have to be converted to Theory Y or Theory Z before this chapter can have any real meaning to managers in general.

At this particular point it is a bit depressing to consider how many Theory X managers are left among our population. They may be a dying breed, but the ones remaining are a particularly hardy lot, and their influence is still tremendously strong throughout the business community. All we can hope for is an early conversion of the unregenerate members of management, with a concomitant chance for business to exercise its proper influence on the social evolution of our country.

HOW DO WE BALANCE THESE DEBTS?

In addition to the difficult tasks of remembering and fulfilling his duties to his people and his company, the manager has a third area of concern: assuring that he always keeps these two debts in balance. Of course, if the social needs of employees are at all times satisfied and if they are happy about the working situation, we might be tempted to assume that the manager's social duties to the company are satisfied. This is not necessarily so. The manager, as the interface between the people who do the work and the executive echelon of the enterprise, still must make sure, first, that communication is always maintained between these two levels and, second, that neither party acts in a way that is inimical to the welfare of the other.

As already indicated, the first logical step in this balancing act is for the manager to be certain that the people who work for him have a clear, complete understanding of the company's philosophy regarding social duties to the work force and to the community. This can be done only when the manager has gone to the trouble of determining that he is correct in his understanding of what the company's position is. This will of necessity be a continuing monitoring process, since it is not at all unusual for a company's position to change with the evolution of the thinking of top brass. They have the right to change their minds just as anyone else does.

The manager can have no reference point for making value judgments unless he is quite clear about both his own social conscience and what he sees as the present state of our society. Currently, the scene is changing with such rapidity that it is nearly a full-time job just to maintain this kind of overview of our country. Alvin Toffler has made a compelling case for this in his extremely important book *Future Shock,* and this should be required reading for every manager in the country. We must first understand how these outside variables are affecting us before we can hope to adjust to them successfully and keep something like normalcy in our lives.

It is obvious that all levels of management have deep responsibilities in the matter of keeping up with social changes and their impact on both individuals and groups. There really is no particular level at which the onus could be said to be heavier, so *every* manager must be alert to what is going on.

Another major area of responsibility for the manager is to assure himself that the people reporting to him are not developing social traits or attributes inimical to the company's goals. In other words, they cannot be allowed to wander aimlessly across the terrain without some sort of leadership giving them enlightenment about the effect of their social evolution on the course of their employing agency. At the same time, it is clearly the duty of the manager to resist adamantly any change in the employer's social actions which he conceives to be potentially harmful to his people. The word "adamantly" was chosen deliberately. This area is of such deep importance to the manager's career and principles that he must be willing to make an issue of any proposed change if he deems it irrational or harmful to either the company or its work force. Career decisions have been made thousands of times on less critical incidents.

Furthermore, the manager has a personal duty to make sure that his thinking on the social responsibilities of the business community is both rational and comprehensive. It is exceedingly easy to be caught up by fads and passing fancies of the general public, and this must be guarded against as strongly as possible. Under the enthusiasm engendered by a craze of the moment, the manager can do irreparable harm to himself, his people, and his company because of the influence he exerts on those working with him.

It is imperative that we assure ourselves of at least the face validity of any social causes we espouse, lest we fall into a trap very difficult to extricate ourselves from. Our general feelings of goodwill toward those working for us might lead us to pamper them to the point where they lose their independence and their will to work for themselves. The entire populace of our country has been exposed to this general theory for more than two generations; it is a credit to the essentially strong character of our heritage that we have not been totally ruined as individuals and as a population. It is fallacious to expect the government, or business and industry, to take on the entire load, leaving the individual with no responsibility except to lie back and enjoy it.

As much as anything else, the manager's social responsibility on the job, both to his people and to the company, is to work hard at keeping his people aware of their personal debts to themselves, the company, and society at large. It is in maintaining a proper balance among these social duties that the manager will encounter difficulty. Nobody else can really tell him how to do this; it is a personal responsibility which he can neither duck nor successfully delegate to another person. This problem is compounded by the fact that in many cases upper managements of companies have failed to recognize their social duties, thus throwing an intolerable burden on middle and lower managers in trying to keep things squared away.

WHAT DO WE OWE THE PUBLIC?

The manager has one more significant duty in the social area: to determine what he owes to the public. In the final analysis, of course, the manager's social responsibility is to society at large, and not to a limited segment of it as represented by his employers and their enterprise. Unfortunately, this concept is not too widely held in the world of business and industry. But if we are to survive and prosper, it must become the overriding consideration in every manager's thinking about his work. While it may be possible for a small group to prosper at the expense of the many, if this were to be extended universally our entire society would rot and disappear, as have others which lived by the same philosophy.

We can only grow and gain strength if the entire population subscribes to the belief that "the best for the most" should be our governing philosophy. If what we are about to do will benefit more than it will hurt, if our contribution is to the many and not the few, then we have satisfied the basic criterion for the formation of a business organization, and we have a right to survive if our other actions are correct. This belief, and this way of governing our actions, should be the foundation of our thinking and must control every action we take on the job.

The manager who believes this and who orders his life on this basis will of necessity become quite militant in selling his philosophy to his peers and to those managers above and below him in the hierarchy. He must be prepared to do battle seriously with many of his fellows who are as yet unsold on this proposition.

For example, if this attitude and set of actions were wholeheartedly subscribed to by all managers in all industries, the current flurry of activity about dangers to our ecosystem would disappear. Ecological policing would become unnecessary as each industry took care of its own problems of pollution on a voluntary basis. A few individual companies have already accepted this responsibility, with some revolutionary and exciting results. They have learned that a grateful and perceptive public will recognize their actions and that business is substantially better for them because they have chosen this approach.

It is obvious on the face of it that the manager who sees his social duty and does it has a perfect right to demand that others act in the same way. He can with a clear conscience take on any competitor or other organization that acts in a selfish manner inimical to the public good. Actually, as a matter of self-protection the manager will have to do this, or predators among his competition will do him in.

It is *not* necessary to adopt a priggish or holier-than-thou attitude to act under this social duty. This is purely a matter of taking on a decent, responsible way of life and ordering our activities in consonance with it. If we treat others decently, we have a right to expect decent treatment from them.

8

THE MANAGER AND DEVELOPMENTAL ACTIVITIES

All life is a matter of growth and development. Unless we grow physically after birth, our lives will be very short and unproductive, and we will never be anything but a burden to others for the short time of our existence. It is odd that a significant percentage of managerial people fail to see the direct parallel between our physical lives and our careers in management and the work situation in general. This chapter will explore the developmental aspects of the manager's job and how he can make his work easier by paying some close attention to this extremely important activity.

DEVELOPMENT IS A SELF-PROTECTIVE NECESSITY

Because of exposure, because of the jealousies and hatreds of others, and because of the nature of the work itself, a manager is vulnerable to attack in many different facets of the job. Let us consider some of the natural enemies of the manager in the area of self-development and the development of the people who work for and with him.

Item: We have already noted several times the rapidity and fundamental nature of the changes occurring in our social scene, some of them almost from day to day. The manager who values his job can keep it safe only if he stands ready to make the necessary personal adjustments to his surroundings. Making personal changes is a complex process, involving the extinction of old habits and the formation of new ones — always a harrowing thing for the individual involved to contemplate and then to put into effect.

When we contemplate making changes in the work group, we see that this is immensely more complex and difficult, since changes within individuals will concomitantly produce changes in group interactions, requiring the greatest possible expertise on the part of the group leader. So at the very least the manager is under the obligation of producing change within himself, being the agent of change for the rest of the group, and then monitoring and guiding the group process while this change is underway. This is no small job, nor one which can easily be delegated and forgotten about.

Item: The manager is well aware that his peers are undergoing the same process of change that he is managing for himself and his group. If he allows himself to falter in this duty, he is ensuring his eventual failure as a manager, since he will quickly cease to be competitive with other group leaders. As a basic personal philosophical tenet, the successful manager should be ready at all times to put forth the effort to remain a little ahead of his peers in the matter of development and growth. It is not really safe simply to try to "keep up with the Joneses." Here is a case where the goal should be to outstrip the competition as often as possible. If it becomes apparent, as most managers have recently discovered, that you must be fundamentally literate in EDP, then don't fight it, but try as quickly as possible to gain the expertise needed to keep your group up with all others in the enterprise. The same principle applies to any other change seen as necessary.

Item: Your management will expect this of you as a continuing part of your job. This attention to growth and development is a part of the minimum requirements for being a success as a modern manager. Unfortunately for some group leaders, upper echelons sometimes assume this quality and activity so completely that they do not verbalize it to their subordinates, thinking that they will automatically be busying themselves with developmental activities as a natural part of their jobs. Later, when it is discovered that this has not been happening in some cases, it is almost always too late, and we have another managerial casualty.

The best and safest approach, of course, is to initiate communications from time to time with your managers to reassure yourself of their desires in this area. What do they want you to do about developing yourself and others, and how much of it do they want? Once these things have been determined, your job will be to implement the growth and change, and in this part of the job you should have the authority to effect the necessary changes in the manner you think best and most economical.

The management of development is a self-protective activity from a slightly different viewpoint as well. We can never forget that the public (those not connected with our enterprise) often will have an effect on our success or failure as managers. The most obvious group are our customers. There is a curious dichotomy in people's thinking about the things or services that they buy. In some cases they are attracted to a thing or a service because it has been produced almost without change for many years. The Daimler and Rolls Royce cars are cases in point. People will return for generations to a company which can deliver nearly perfect replicas of what their grandfathers got from the same company.

But this is only part of our thinking in this situation. Most of the time our customers are unhappy unless they have the latest thing or the newest service. They want to have all the newest gadgets and improvements which have come along. As managers, then, we must be alert to which of these customer categories our business attracts so that we can determine infallibly how much growth and development will be mandatory for us personally, and for our people as individuals and as a group.

SELF-DEVELOPMENT

The manager cannot logically call on his people to take an interest in developmental activities unless he is himself involved in a continual growth situation. Our society has evolved in such a way that nobody can keep up with the parade of events without continual effort at new learning and adult-education activities.

There are three major stages in any program of self-development. The first is to take an objective inventory of your assets and liabilities as a manager. Because of your membership in the minority group of managers, there are some special requirements that other workers do not have. This introspective self-evaluation takes a kind of discipline many people are unused to, and it must be done thoroughly (and on an ongoing basis) to be effective for your needs. The process begins by setting down a list of traits, attributes, abilities, knowledges, and skills which you feel are necessary on your job. Then comes an estimate of where you stand on each of these needs at the present moment. Are you in the middle of the spectrum for this need? On the low side? Way above the average? When you have totaled up your balance sheet for the list you have developed, it is always wise to counsel with someone else for whom you have a lot of respect and get his or her estimate of your position for each item on your list. Any large discrepancies between your evaluations and those of your counselor should be talked over thoroughly until close agreement is reached.

This inventory then becomes the blueprint for the second step in self-development: the planning of your development over a time continuum. Remember not to make the grave error of ignoring your strengths in planning for your growth. The wise manager will work at least as hard on his strengths as he will on his weaknesses, just as an athlete will concentrate on those activities in which he does the best if he wants to be a winner. Another point to keep in mind is that it is fatal to try to do too many things over a discrete time period, such as a year. It is far better to plan for—and achieve—three or four items than it is to scatter your energies over six or eight things and not accomplish any of them well.

In planning for your self-development, remind yourself constantly of the many methods there are for achieving personal growth. For example, colleges and universities offer many formal courses in management, some of them only a few days in length, others such as MBA programs running for one or two years. There are many advantages to attending one of these "public" groups, not the least of which is exposure to the thinking and experiences of your peers.

Trade associations and professional groups often sponsor developmental activities for their members. These have the advantage of being tailored to the problems and situations peculiar to these special groups, and their relevancy can be quite high.

Independent study (correspondence courses) has experienced a mushroom growth during the past few years. There are literally hundreds of well-developed programs on a huge diversity of subjects available to the independent student. The local librarian can usually be helpful in running down your particular sphere of interest and locating the course you need. Directly associated with independent study is a relatively new technique which has enjoyed a rapid growth during the past fifteen years: programmed instruction. With this method, the student gets immediate feedback about his progress, and there is no long wait to learn whether a response was right or wrong. The one drawback is the high cost of developing good courses in PI.

Another relatively new method of instruction is the use of audio or video cassette tapes. Many programs are being put on tape and some of them are of high quality. The major limitation is the high cost, especially of the video cassettes.

Many managers find it useful to look for others with similar needs and interests and then to organize a study group. It is not necessary to have a leader for this sort of activity, although some groups feel a little uncomfortable if there is nobody to lean on for support when they have questions.

However, it should be remembered that 90 percent or more of a manager's development will occur right on the job. The key is to be alert for learning experiences while at work and to profit from them. Obviously, your boss should be enlisted in the process right at the start and should be called upon often for advice and counsel.

The third and most crucial step in the process of self-development is to implement the plan you come up with. We need to reinforce here the thesis that too much attempted will ruin the entire effort. Remember you still have your job to do, and it must not suffer because you are gone too much or have your attention riveted on developmental activities to the exclusion of your everyday work problems. Careful consideration of your working calendar will usually tell you how you can space your self-developmental efforts to your best advantage, so that your learning will be optimal.

One last, but vital, point should always be remembered: The first and most important reason for self-development is *improvement on your present job.* It is extremely difficult to plan a self-development program which will directly prepare you for advancement, for you cannot be truly certain to what job you will be promoted. On the other hand, it is relatively easy to determine what things will help you to do better where you now are, and high performance on your present job is the only real basis for your being picked for advancement. Once promoted, you can grow into that job just as you have grown and developed in your present one.

DEVELOPMENT OF SUBORDINATES

As stated previously, in the matter of developmental activities the manager owes a duty not only to himself but also to his subordinates. In other words, managerial responsibility is toward the growth of the group, both as a group and as a sum of the individuals comprising it. One of the easiest traps to fall into is to expect every member of the group to develop at the same rate. The tidy manager would, of course, like to see his people growing and increasing their capabilities together, but this is an impossible dream. Each of us has a different growth and maturation rate; each of us will grow more quickly in some areas than some of our peers; each of us will develop more slowly in other areas than those around us.

By all odds the easiest and best way for a manager to discharge his duty in the area of developing his subordinates is to install some form of Management by Objectives. When this is done, and when the proper follow-up is observed, there can be measurable and concrete advances according to predetermined goals agreed upon by the manager and each employee. The cycle is relatively simple in concept. The first stage is to rewrite a viable position description for the person concerned. There is an amazing amount of misunderstanding between employees and their managers about what the true nature of the job is. In more than half the cases researched, the jobholder and his boss had significant differences in their understanding of the scope of authority the worker had. Unless a complete meeting of the minds is achieved, the entire process becomes sterile and fruitless. The best procedure is for both the manager and the employee to write a position description for the job, compare them, and negotiate the differences until understanding is achieved.

The next step is to negotiate a set of objectives for the jobholder to achieve in a discrete time interval—say, six months or a year. The trick here is not to pick too many items or too many areas for improvement at one time. Both parties should keep in mind that the objectives must be neither too easy nor too difficult to reach. It is best to set objectives which will stretch the subject, so that there will be a real feeling of accomplishment when they are reached, but not to make them impossible, or the process will be self-defeating. Frequent checkups should be scheduled, so that both parties know exactly where the subject stands at any given moment.

The success of the entire venture lies in the fact that the objectives must be renegotiable right up to the last day, should an intervening variable arise which the worker cannot control and which might threaten the attainment of the goal. This is only fair, and nobody should be criticized for failure to reach an objective for reasons beyond his sphere of control.

The last step in the cycle is to have a performance review at the end of the agreed-upon time. There is significant difference between the MBO review and the traditional performance review. Under MBO, the subject is the one who does most of the talking. The boss limits his talking to questions or to requests for necessary documentation. It is to be noted that the entire atmosphere of the MBO performance review is different from the old kind. The subject is relaxed; he speaks from his own personal knowledge; he feels that the process has been as objective as it is possible for any human interaction to be. A final aspect of the process is that room should be allowed not only for having achieved the agreed-upon objectives but for rewarding excellent performance above and beyond the original objectives.

Managing the development of subordinates is not an easy process at first. Two key danger points have already been noted: writing a realistic position description known to both parties and setting objectives which are difficult, but not impossible, to achieve. Concomitant with the performance review, the entire matter should be recycled by negotiating some new objectives (which naturally will be a little more difficult than the preceding ones). Managers should also be aware that the ideal situation exists when an entire organization is operating under MBO, with real support from the top of the hierarchy. Under these conditions, the enterprise has a chance for splendid progress and meaningful achievements. However, if top management does not buy the idea of MBO as a company philosophy, any manager can still install it for his own group; in other words, it can be self-contained within any department.

Methodologies will be the same at practically all levels. Self-development is self-development, wherever it occurs. Naturally, the areas to be worked on will differ from person to person, but the same methods and routes are open to all members of the organization, irrespective of their levels in the ladder. To be specific, colleges and universities usually have offerings designed for all levels of the organization, from pre-supervisory candidates through supervision, middle manage-ment, and executive echelons. The same is true to a greater or lesser extent for the other methods of development pre-viously discussed.

The role of the manager in the development of subordinates is, first, to assure himself of the motivation of his employees to grow and develop and, second, to be certain that he is offer-ing leadership, time, counsel, and help all along the way for those working for him. He can never afford to let up in this activity, for it is the nerve center of the entire organization. Once established and underway, it will become just like any other facet of the managerial job — not easy, certainly, but one which can be attained and from which obvious benefits will accrue.

DEVELOPMENT IS AN ONGOING PROCESS

The thesis that the manager's developmental duties are on-going needs to be thoroughly reinforced. The nature of competi-tion in business and industry is such that any manager who fails to keep both himself and his people "up with the times" is doomed to failure. Taken from either an external or an internal viewpoint, the competition is fierce and unremitting and be-comes a simple matter of survival. The organization is always in competition with other enterprises, and businesses make it or break it according to the caliber of their management. Tech-nology is at such a state that any company can put out a viable product; the management is the element which instills the necessary muscular tonus to keep the business going and healthy.

No manager can safely be unaware of the nature and ex-pertise of his opposite numbers in competitive companies. He should study them closely for their strengths and weak-nesses, just as he studies himself and his people for the same attributes. One thing should be remembered: It is extremely dangerous to try to compete with a rival in his special areas of strength unless you are strong in the same areas. The thing to do here is to surpass him by using your own special talents to the utmost—in other words, beat him where you are strong and he is weak. If this sounds like life in the jungle, so be it.

The observation and study of external competition will take some doing. It will mean accepting the challenge of the time involved, plus exercising considerable ingenuity in order to get the data necessary to understand and evaluate your rivals. This is *not* to say that you will be forced to engage in industrial espionage in order to get your information; it does mean that you will have to alert yourself to what is going on among rival companies by studying the external evidence and analyzing the human elements behind this performance. Actually, most managers have considerable contact with their peers in other companies through professional and trade associations, chambers of commerce, and similar groups. Your peers, of course, will be studying you in a similar manner, so the total arrangement is a fair and equitable one.

Studying your competition within the company presents a somewhat different challenge. Although we all know of instances where managers have risen to success over the bodies of their peers and superiors, we also know that this is a dangerous way to go and one which in the long run is to be strongly discouraged. You will have much more need for friends and colleagues among your peers than you will have for enemies. Enough of the latter are generated without your wishes or against your planning.

Once again, however, the knowledgeable manager is aware that he must be intimately acquainted with the state of development of his peers, subordinates, and superiors at any given instant. It is completely acceptable to scout your competition in the same way that professional athletic teams scout their rivals. In fact, there is no necessity even to keep this activity a secret; everyone does it, and everyone knows that others are doing it on a day-to-day basis.

The same caution exists here as in scouting your external competition: You must be aware of particular strengths and weaknesses in all your peers, subordinates, and superiors. It is best not to challenge the champ in a given function unless you have ample reason to think that you are at least as strong as he or she is in this activity.

It is obvious that it will be much easier to get the necessary data for your internal competitors than for those on the outside. The evidence is much closer to home and much more overt than it is in another enterprise. The danger here is that we all tend to overlook and underestimate the familiar in our daily lives. Because we know that a peer is very much a human being, we may seriously underestimate his overall strength. That is why a "dark horse" quite often zips to the top of the heap, in business as well as in athletic competition. The answer, of course, is that this person has been assiduously attending to his own development, while maintaining a low profile until the time is at hand for displaying his true expertise. Everyone is aware that a superior sense of timing can make a champion in any field of endeavor. In the long-distance races, the winner usually lets someone else pace him until the last lap or so when he makes his big push.

While all of this is going on, the manager must also cultivate an awareness of the state of development of those below him and above him in the hierarchy. One word of caution here. It is never a good idea to be jealous or afraid of one of your own people. If a member of your crew shows potential greater than your own, the worst thing you can do is to try to block his progress. Far better to turn to him and offer every help you can. Most certainly, it would not be bad to have the president of the company remember how you helped him on the road up. In fact, the more friends you have in high places, the better for your own secure and upwardly mobile future in the company and the industry. Much the same thing can be said for developing a subordinate who later leaves the organization for a big jump in another company. It is good to have cordial relations with the key people in your competition. Who knows when and how they may be willing, even anxious, to return your earlier favors?

DEVELOPMENTAL TOOLS

The manager will find, as he lives with the philosophy and practice of developing himself and his people, that it is becoming significantly harder to stay abreast, almost day by day. As our technology proliferates and as our social structure undergoes some deep and fundamental changes, it becomes more and more difficult to adjust ourselves individually to these changes, just as the group is exhibiting some new and different characteristics.

For one thing, our developmental tools are becoming vastly more sophisticated each year. Two examples of current developmental processes will serve to illustrate the point. There has been a great deal of activity recently in the area of sensitivity training (T-groups) for managers. Thousands of managers have been exposed to this extremely controversial technique over the past couple of decades. The theory holds that a person undergoing this experience will become more sensitive to his impact on those around him and will be better able to adjust his behavior to their needs and demands. In some people this seems to be the case; in others a deep and devastating trauma is produced which may have unfortunate effects on their careers and on them as individuals. Instead of becoming more sensitive to their environment, these people may turn into neurotic introverts who find it even harder to adjust.

Another new technique which has enjoyed wide popularity in recent years is simulation, or management games. When properly designed, and especially when computerized, these games can be an excellent teaching tool of managerial theory. In a few days' time management teams can run through a simulation of a quarter or even a year of business "experience," with nearly instant feedback on the correctness or incorrectness of their decisions. In addition, there is a great amount of ego involvement among the members of the various teams; they become intensely interested in "winning" for their group. If the proper facilities are available, these games can be played before or after working hours, with no need to be gone from work at all.

As stated, these two illustrations are drawn from a swiftly increasing body of new developmental techniques for the members of management. Now the problem is one of making the wisest choice among them for the training and education of a manager in his particular areas of need. This choice becomes more critical when we realize how much the costs of training and education have escalated. The use of developmental tools is also costly, as we have all been finding out.

It would seem unnecessary to put in a plug for the manager to become aware of and explore the behavioral sciences, yet we must do so for those who might not be thinking in this direction. The thesis could be defended vigorously that the manager of tomorrow will be unable to operate effectively unless he is literate in this field, if for no other reason than that those people who will be working for him will also have knowledge in the behavioral sciences. The boss who allows his people to be better informed than he is, is unnecessarily handicapping himself and is courting disaster. In the future this will be particularly true in the area of labor-management interactions; the international unions are well aware of the behavioral sciences and what knowledge of these sciences can do for them in negotiations and in day-to-day living in plants and offices.

To recapitulate, the matter of developing both himself and his people has become of top-grade importance to today's manager, and that importance is not about to diminish in the future. The man or woman who bears the leadership responsibility in a work group must be ready to face up to this matter of development and take it on as a major part of the managerial job. Of critical importance to the manager's performance in this area is the extent and kind of planning done, both for individuals and for the group. If the group consists of ten or more people, the manager would do well to construct and use a PERT time chart as a control on the developmental process. Follow-up is of extreme importance in this activity; the best planning in the world will be useless unless the manager monitors what is actually going on.

In planning and monitoring the developmental process, the manager will find that an immense amount of coordination is needed. It is essential that developmental activities for individuals be integrated for the most economical use of their time and the company's money. Savings of significant size can be realized by grouping people with similar needs and then using one go-round of activity for all of them. The manager should also remember to make full use of the experts in the field, either in-house or on the outside. Directors of management development or organizational development are there to perform a service; it would be foolish not to make use of their expertise. Naturally, the manager's own line of command should be closely consulted at each major step to ensure agreement with proposed plans of action.

Of one thing we can be sure: The manager who does a good job in self-development and in assisting the development of his subordinates will find in this some of the more deeply rewarding experiences of managerial life.

9

PEER RELATIONSHIPS OF THE MANAGER

It should be obvious that the way a manager relates with others is largely conditioned by his basic philosophy. If he believes deeply that it is his duty to get along well with others, he will tend to make that happen. Conversely, if he feels that getting his way is the most important part of his business life, he will probably have many abrasive interactions with those around him, particularly with his equals, for they too will have their ambitions and unattained objectives.

WHEN DO YOU NOT KEEP THE PEACE?

Whatever sort of philosophy may be guiding your actions, there are inevitably times when you will find it impossible to avoid confrontations and direct clashes with your peers. One situation which demands this is when a peer's behavior is dysfunctional, dishonest, or immoral. In this case, you have no choice but to challenge his actions and take him on, no matter how strong he may be or how entrenched his position in the organization is. This is the kind of battle which is necessary, and it must be resolved definitively, because the position is untenable. The best part of your situation here is that you will automatically have as allies all the "good guys," and you will never have to defend your position to those who count.

A second situation which demands confrontation is when you are under direct attack by another manager or a group of them. We are talking here not of the perfectly natural rivalry which exists among peers but of the appearance of active hostility accompanied by an overt attempt to harm you in your career. Under these circumstances, you would be less than human if you did not respond with aggressive behavior. Moreover, you would be smart to alert your own line of managers to what is going on, so that they will not be surprised to learn of the conflict later.

A third case which calls for action on your part is when your peers refuse you the cooperation necessary to get your job done. While nothing overt may happen, they may sabotage you pretty thoroughly by failing to do for you that part of their job which affects your work. Here again, you will have to involve at least one higher echelon of management in both your department and others so that all concerned will know what is going on. This action on the part of your peers is perhaps the hardest kind of hostility to document, because there are always so many plausible-sounding reasons for their failure to cooperate at a crucial moment. You should be aware of the fact that some managers become very adept at covering their tracks with false documentation, such as "copies" to the file of memos which were never sent to anyone else. It may be difficult to convince other managers of what you know in your heart to be the truth of the matter.

Fourth in this series of hypothetical situations is when other managers make a raid on your people, either to pirate them to their group or to bypass your line of authority to get something they want done. If there is ever a time when you will have to assert your authority, this is it. If you do not, you can only lose the respect of the peer involved *and* of your own people. They will expect a leader to lead. Of course, if the relationship between you and your people is what it should be, they will tell you immediately when your peer enemy is making his move. If they do not, you have some extensive repair work to do in your house. Once more, you are the boss in your area, and everyone working for you must acknowledge this basic fact of life.

A fifth occasion which calls for action on your part is when you discover one of your peers to be doing something inimical to the good of the organization, whether or not it affects you directly. Of course, in the long run it *will* affect you directly, so the sooner you get into this act, the better for all concerned. This much you owe to your employers as a condition of employment. Depending on the facts of the individual case, there may or may not be a need for publicity. It could be such that you would act and never tell anyone else about it. Sometimes simply confronting the miscreant with your knowledge of what is going on will be enough to correct his behavior before irreparable damage has been done.

Naturally, this list does not exhaust all possible cases when you would disrupt the peace with one or more of your peers. It should be enough, however, to indicate that simply because you are in management things will inevitably occur which will call for some direct action on your part. People being what they are, there will always be some conflict on the working scene, and it is the manager's duty to take care of it. In each of the cases mentioned, it is a managerial responsibility to *initiate* conflict as the only viable method of resolving the problem. Lest we leave the wrong impression, it is still true that the average manager will discover, thankfully, that a vast majority of his peer relationships will be good rather than bad. Most of the people in management—at least those who last—are men and women of basic goodwill. If this were not so, nobody in his right mind could stand a lifetime in management.

WHAT DO YOU OWE YOUR COLLEAGUES?

Philosophically, you assumed certain duties to your peers the day you became a manager, and these are ongoing and unremitting. First and foremost, you owe them respect—for as long as they continue to earn it. Actually to be a member of management should be a source of pride to you, since you have been picked to represent a small minority of the work force. You expect respect from your peers; you owe it to them just as certainly. This mutual respect among the leaders of the work force is the only basis on which management can eventually become a true profession.

Second, you owe your peers help and cooperation. When attitudes and actions are ideal, little thought is given to whether these actions are spelled out specifically in your job description. The fact that a peer needs your help and cooperation is the key, rather than any written dictate in your position description. With the increasing complexity of our social and business organizations, this matter of freely given cooperation becomes more important, almost on a day-to-day basis. You have by this time discovered that you need it from others; they too need your help often. A little planning will allow you to work a comfortable amount of help and cooperation with others into your daily schedule, and there should be little trouble in performing in this area.

Third, you owe your colleagues advice and counsel, *both when they ask for it and sometimes when they don't.* It is a human trait to shy away from certain areas in which we have weaknesses. We don't like to face up to our trouble spots, and we just may have to be jogged by another person to make us do this at all. If you have strength and expertise in a given area of management, it is your plain duty to share that with other managers less gifted in that part of the job. After all, you had a lot of help from others on your way up, and you can't evade returning these favors sometime later.

However, this is a long way from being *only* altruistic. You gain in strength and maturity every time you give help to a peer. You become a better and wiser manager each time you offer counsel to another. The one thing absolutely necessary in this context is to be continually aware of the cues given by your peers that your advice and counsel are needed. Many times, of course, they will ask you for it directly, and this becomes easy. The difficult times occur when they give you evidence of their need but are not fully aware of it themselves.

It is then that you must be particularly sensitive and approach the situation carefully and diplomatically.

Fourth, you owe your colleagues a willingness to be of service to the people who work for them, at least if they approach you with a request for such help. Remember, the compartmentalization of the management job is artificial and is purely for making the management job definitive. Your managerial duties will in almost every case extend beyond the limits of your particular group, and you will find yourself giving service for varying lengths of time to people who report to other managers. Remember, when you accede to requests of this sort from other managers, you will be building relationships with others whom normally you would have little contact with, and this can never be anything but good. The more people we can forge bonds of friendship with, the more secure will be our position in the enterprise, and this is no little matter for any manager.

Fifth, you owe your colleagues clear, intelligible, and complete communication. You expect the word from them to help your work; they most surely have at least as much coming from you. We all know that the gravest and most widespread managerial sin is a failure to communicate properly. There are many reasons for this. We all like to possess classified information, but many times this information is necessary to another manager's operations. In addition, many managers make fallacious assumptions about the state of information of their peers. They assume that everyone knows something when obviously this is not true. It is far better to repeat something that *is* known than to withhold something that is not universally known. Of course, it is never defensible to withhold information in the desire to hurt another manager. Our likes or dislikes of others as persons are not germane to our duties here.

Sixth, it is your clear obligation to be loyal to your peers in their times of trouble. Any way you look at it, the manager's job is one of continual, unremitting pressure. Each of us reacts a little differently to this pressure, and when it gets to be a little much our peers should rally round and be supportive until control is reestablished. In short, each of us is grateful for the help and loyalty of our friends when the going gets sticky.

In summation, it would seem that the manager owes to his peers the same efforts that he would like them to expend in his direction. The true manager should be mature enough not to be embarrassed by living under the Golden Rule. It has proved viable for a couple of thousand years, and that should be good enough for anyone.

WHAT CAN YOU EXPECT FROM YOUR PEERS?

The simplistic answer to what you can expect from your peers is that you can expect exactly what you are prepared to give them in your interpersonal relations. But we should examine this question more closely, because it is a very human characteristic to expect *more* than we are usually prepared to give, and this we have to guard against. Perhaps we can run through a short list of specifics and look at them in the light of what is reasonable to expect from all our peers.

The first concern might logically be honesty. We could say that it is reasonable to expect complete and total honesty from our peers at all times, but this is eminently not so. There are many reasons why your opposite numbers will not completely level with you. For one thing, to do so might cause them trouble, and in that case it is usually not realistic to expect the average person to be *completely* truthful. He will most certainly look for a way to hedge that will get him off the hook and forestall the troublesome situation.

Another case where you might expect a little doctoring of the truth is when the absolute verities involved might be harmful or upsetting to you. This happens especially when you are talking with a peer who is well disposed toward you and who doesn't want to hurt your feelings. Most of us find no difficulty in rationalizing the "white lies" we tell others to save their feelings, and almost everyone does so at some time or another. We must always be on the lookout for this. You might also get less than complete honesty from your peers when total knowledge would give you an advantage over them in the industrial jungle. No person in his right mind would willingly give a competitor a better chance of "making it" than he has himself. We would be unreasonable to expect this to happen.

A second major concern is how much cooperation you can look for from your peers. This is ordinarily governed by two things: their feelings toward you and the amount of extra labor involved for them or their crews in offering you the help you need. Again, most of us have a tendency to want and expect more cooperation from our peers than is reasonable. We forget how often we have turned down a colleague's request because it would have required us to go an extra mile, rather than the half-mile we are usually prepared to travel. Once more, we find no difficulty, nor do we lose any sleep, in refusing such a request, and we should be neither surprised nor hurt when our peers behave exactly toward us as we do toward them.

The same factor is operative here as in the matter of honesty: Your peer may decide that to cooperate to the extent that you are asking would give you an unfair advantage over him, and you know what the answer will be if he thinks that. We have a tendency to maintain two sets of standards as to how much extra we can ask from our people as compared to what we think a peer should ask from his people in helping us, and those standards are likely to be loaded in our favor, no matter how much we think we are fair, reasonable, and objective. Our world today is immensely complex and complicated, but it is still built from the goals, actions, expectations, and hopes of millions of individuals, and for each of them, of course, their own welfare must come first.

A third major concern is how much you can reasonably expect from your peers in the matter of communication. The one thing you must always remember is that communication skill varies widely among the population, from those few who are nearly perfectly articulate to the few who find it immensely difficult to express anything to others. Thus, even if all our peers were equally friendly to us as individuals, which of course they are not, we should expect great variation in the amount of data forthcoming from different members of our peer group.

Take, for example, the conditioning effect of the respect a colleague has for you. The more he respects you, the less he may communicate to you in the everyday business situation, simply because he will overestimate the amount of your knowledge of what is going on. He may do you a disservice because he thinks so much of you! We must always remember that few managers are inclined to overcommunicate; the vast majority of them sin in the other direction. It then is *not* reasonable for you to expect a great deal of communication from an average peer, even if he feels quite warmly toward you. Whatever you do get from your colleagues will come ordinarily as a result of the artfulness with which you pursue them and dig out what you need.

Finally, how much support can you reasonably expect from your colleagues when you are in a bad spot? Be careful, now! The key word is "reasonably." One more time, our personal bias can easily trip us up here. We may find it next to impossible to be objective enough to measure with any kind of certainty how much support we give when they are in trouble as against what we would expect from them when we are in difficulty. However, in this area we are particularly under the control of the personal regard in which we are held by our colleagues. The more they like us, naturally, the more supportive they will be and the further they will go to render assistance.

In any event, the rational manager will remember that it is suicide to count heavily on the efforts of others to extricate himself from trouble spots which he creates by his own misdirected efforts. Oh, of course, we all build up certain credits in the managerial bank of goodwill, but these credits are acutely subject to an overdraft if we count too greatly on them. In the final analysis, every manager will have to ascertain for himself in any specific situation what is reasonable in his expectations from his peers.

PEER-GROUP RELATIONSHIPS

The peer-group relationships will determine the health of the organization in the main. Unbridled and uncontrolled competitiveness will bring the enterprise to a screeching halt within a short time. Jealousies become cancerous if they are allowed to go without therapy. We are speaking, of course, not only of the one-to-one relationships among the members of a single group of managers but of the interfaces among various groups of peers as well.

The foremost necessity for all managers in an enterprise is to establish a climate of mutual supportiveness. The reasons for forming a managerial group should never be forgotten: These are the overall objectives of the company, and their achievement is the basic duty of every manager in the concern. Only when the entire organization is healthy and functioning can individual managers expect to be successful and to achieve their personal goals. If a particular group is observed to be slacking off in its efforts at supporting other groups, it is up to all other managers to take corrective action. The sooner the change in attitude is identified, the sooner everyone can collaborate on turning around the managers concerned and getting them back on the proper track.

It must be recognized that this effort will never be an easy one, and the managers striving to correct the problem must be ready to take strong measures, as well as to be prepared for rebuffs and initial failures. As splinter groups appear among the managers, top echelons will have to assume their strongest posture of leadership and show by their actions and examples the right way to go. This is not always a simple matter, because the defectors will have personal reasons for not going along with the rest of management, and it may be exceedingly difficult to convince them that they are wrong.

A second necessity for the winning enterprise is that the various management groups be intuitive in anticipating the needs of others. All of us try to do this for our own wants and needs, but the professional manager will have to go further and include others in this part of his job. In essence, this is a portion of his managerial planning, especially his long-range planning. We can never plan for ourselves completely without including at least partially the activities of others outside our group, because no management division is ever completely self-contained. This interdependence of management within an organization is increasing and will continue to grow in the foreseeable future. A natural fallout of this growing complexity is a need for cooperation among all groups of managers in the anticipation of future needs or the preparation for inevitable change.

A final necessity for any true manager is a complete and unreserved responsiveness to calls for his special expertise by other functions. There was a day not too long past when the various disciplines of a company could go very nearly their own way, each contributing a discrete facet to the overall work of the enterprise. That day is gone forever. Company finance is no longer an esoteric, ingrown specialty to be understood only by finance people. Data processing can no longer be a jealously guarded secret by its practitioners; on the contrary, it is their clear duty to get actively into the job of enlightening their fellow managers about what EDP can do for them. Engineering today affects every aspect of the work done by other managers. Manufacturing and quality control can no longer afford the luxury of hatred and strife; their mutual well-being is totally interlocked, and neither can succeed without the other.

Purchasing departments have changed to procurement agencies, and they know, if they are up to date on their jobs, that their function is actually consultative rather than dictatorial. Methods and systems people must become aware of the behavioral sciences, and they must recognize the human needs of all employees, rather than being concerned only with "efficiency." The latter term can be grossly misleading, if all that is considered are the "thing" processes or mechanical aspects of the operations of the company. The human variable is too critical to let this go on any longer.

What we are saying is that today's and tomorrow's managers must become intensely aware of and continue to study the interactions which take place daily within the management team, and they must strive constantly to improve these relations on a steady upward plane. The survival of any given enterprise, as well as the survival of American business and industry, depends upon our managerial acuteness in these areas. Our competitors in other countries and other continents are well aware of these facts, and they are swiftly becoming expert in the nuances and shadings of peer-group relationships. The next few years will determine whether America will remain a world leader or even a major power in the industrial world, and this will be governed by how well the American manager undertakes the complicated but fascinating study of peer-group dynamics. This will make or break us, beginning right now.

10

DUTIES TO THE ENTERPRISE vs. DUTIES TO SELF

From the nature of his job, the manager is automatically in a dichotomous situation. Vectors on the job will conflict with his own wants and needs; sometimes they will actually become harmful to the manager unless proper steps are taken to alleviate pressure situations. A manager may discover suddenly that what started out as a thrilling challenge has become a drag and a heavy load, simply because there are inherent parts of the managerial job which generate trauma and cause dissatisfaction.

WHAT CAN CREATE A CONFLICT SITUATION?

One of the most common complaints of the manager is that the job involves too much of his time. Few managers can work eight hours a day and get the job done. They find themselves staying at the office long after the people working for them have gone home. Or, if they do leave for home, they take along a heavy briefcase of papers which will demand their attention when they get there. Many a manager discovers that he doesn't have enough time for his family. His children are growing up as strangers to him, and his wife must make a life for herself apart from his activities. The rationalization that the extra work will provide many niceties for the family, luxuries which would otherwise be unattainable, just doesn't quite solve the basic problem.

The tyranny of time in the manager's life goes beyond this. He doesn't have time for his own needs and for personal activities which have been important to him before. Old hobbies and skills have been so neglected that they are no longer sources of pleasure, but only nostalgic memories. A hard, persistent study of the use of his time may pay some dividends by improving his working methods, but the odds are high that this will continue to be a source of irritation for as long as he is in the job.

A second area of concern for the manager is that the accumulated pressures from the job may have adverse effects on his health. Many companies have come to realize this and have established "executive health programs" which offer such benefits as regular physical examinations, enforced longer vacations, the delegation of more of the manager's job to his subordinates, and the encouragement of various kinds of relaxing physical hobbies such as golf and tennis.

The fact remains that most of this physical disruption occurs from the mental stresses on the job, rather than from hard physical labor. This means that the most viable attack on the problem is to try to reduce these mental and emotional stresses, rather than to treat them symptomatically. In other words, reduce the causes of the problem before it becomes serious. Many companies employ psychologists as staff people, and they can often give good counsel to the managerial members of the organization who are finding their pressures insupportable. Today our mental health and our physical health are equally important, simply because they are usually closely intertwined and affect one another.

A third common source of psychological trouble for the manager is when he discovers that company policy has been so altered that he can no longer agree with it as a matter of principle. This is a real tragedy when it occurs, because by this time the manager has probably invested a major part of his working life and his energies in the company. He has a stake in it which is too big to be tossed away lightly. A basic change in company policy is upsetting to the manager psychologically because it is an evidence that he doesn't have as much influence on top management as he once did, or at least as much as he thought he did. Such a realization is extremely upsetting and threatening to the manager, perhaps even as much as the discovery of changes which are antithetical to his beliefs. It will also lead to a great deal of wheelspinning and loss of efficiency on his part while he is trying to think through his problem and find a way out of it. Nobody can tell a particular manager when he has reached the critical point; he is the only one capable of making this decision.

A fourth source of discomfiture to the manager arises from personality clashes with higher management. It would be silly to deny that these can and do occur, and they will cause trouble for the manager lower in the hierarchy. In this case, he can expect that his work will not be as well received as if he had a good relationship with the man upstairs. More occasions will be found to criticize; fewer achievements will be given their full recognition. When this happens in a medium-sized or large company there is one small gleam of relief: The managerial makeup is subject to quite rapid change. Maybe your position or that of your enemy will be different in a relatively short time, and things will be better.

Many managers discover to their sorrow that their employment in a given company can put them into conflict with the community in which they live. Large corporations of almost any sort are likely to be suspect by the general public. We have a fairly long heritage of fear and distrust of what the "giants" will do to the communities where they operate. Unfortunately, until the most recent times there was often more than a degree of truth backing up this distrust. Now, however, most major companies are making an honest effort to clean up their reputations by taking a closer look at their effect on their surroundings and correcting whatever damage may have occurred. Today most managers can honestly meet their neighbors with the knowledge that their employers are trying hard to be good citizens, so that there is no need to be apologetic to anyone because they work at a given place.

WHEN DO YOU BLOW THE WHISTLE?

The principal question for every manager is, of course, how far to go in a situation which generates severe conflict between his personal needs and the demands of the employer. We must remember that basic principle does not have to be involved in order for conflict to arise. It may be that company management has decided that the manager is indispensable in the job presently occupied, thus blocking promotion for that individual and causing frustration. A man or woman who has invested twenty years or so in a career with a given employer is going to be extremely hesitant actually to blow the whistle and leave the company. A long search will be made for ways to escape from the entrapment without really severing the relationship.

However, a company that makes this kind of judgment about an individual can expect to lose that employee eventually unless some sort of relief is provided so that the employee can again attain upward mobility. Every manager has a right to continue to advance so far as his ability and performance will carry him, with no roadblocks put in his way by the employer. It is amazing how many companies still do not recognize the personal rights of their management people and how many times they will take discriminatory action against managers at all levels.

As previously stated, it is always possible that a sudden and radical change in overall company policy will cause conflict situations for members of management at the lower levels. The problem here is that too often major policy shifts are conceptualized, discussed at the executive level, and instituted without a proper—or perhaps without even any—discussion of the prospective change with lower levels of managers. This can never be anything but a serious error. There can be no possible reason for implementing a 180-degree shift in major policy without asking for the inputs of all levels of management. If major changes are put in whimsically, or without thorough exploration by all concerned, executives should not be surprised if they lose a large number of their most valuable employees, as much because they have not been consulted as because their conflict is too great to endure. Once an employee is a member of management, he or she has a right to expect to be treated as a manager *all the time.*

In general, the manager who is successful must cultivate a fine sense of discrimination and be able to make valid judgments in situations which apparently put the employer and the individual employee at odds. Is there a real conflict arising from the situation, or is the manager being hypersensitive about the personal effects of a new action by top management? Is he overestimating the possible damage inherent in an executive decision? Should he wait a little while to see what actually will happen as a result of the decision, or must he take immediate action to avoid the expected bad results? These are the sorts of balancing acts every manager must perform many times in a business career, and only one person can make the final decision: the manager involved.

The one situation intolerable to almost every manager is when he makes the considered decision that the executive echelon is deliberately setting out to manipulate lower levels of management. Such cold-blooded and nefarious actions are not unknown in American business and industry, and when they occur they should be strongly challenged immediately by the manager involved. It is entirely possible that a proposed action is just a ploy—a movement made to test lower-level managers to see how tolerant they are of poor treatment by their superiors. Once those involved have shown unmistakable signs of spirit and an intention of defending themselves, top management may retreat and drop the proposed action. However, even if this does happen, there is quite likely to be a residue of bitterness created by the fact that a bad decision came close to being implemented at the expense of one or more members of management. This kind of game playing can be very destructive of managerial morale and loyalty to the company. It hardly ever is worth the risks involved and almost always boomerangs.

It is also possible for the actions of colleagues to put a manager into a conflict situation concerning his needs and those of the company. A proposal by a peer in another area may have less than desirable implications for a given manager. In his judgment, the results of the action may be deleterious to his group and to him personally.

There is a natural sequence of steps for the manager to follow if this contretemps arises. To begin with, he should apprise his peer of his thoughts concerning the proposal. It is always possible that the other manager simply has not thought through the likely consequences of his actions, and he might be glad to drop the change when shown what would happen. If, however, he listens but doesn't hear and indicates that he is going to carry on with his proposal, the manager concerned must carry his fight up the line — in all probability up two lines, if his peer opponent is in another department or reports to different management. At some point there will be a manager or executive who can adjudicate the problem and claim authority over both managers involved.

The main lesson here is that every manager must be ready and willing to make judgments and decisions in situations where his personal needs and desires conflict with those of the company. Unless *he* stands ready to defend himself adequately, it is unlikely that anyone else will do it for him.

RESOLVING CONFLICTS OF INTEREST

Naturally, the manager who finds his own convictions to be at odds with the objectives of his company is in the kind of bind he wants to avoid or at least get out of quickly. It is an untenable situation, both for him and for his employers.

Perhaps the first method considered by most managers for resolving this problem is to change their own value sets and principles. This is at first blush a weak and cowardly thing to do, but we should always remember how much a manager has invested in the time he has spent with the company and how much his future means to both him and his family. He knows for a near certainty that if he bulls his way through and fails to change, almost without exception he will be the loser, perhaps even to the extent of losing his job and having to make another start. These considerations are enough to make anyone stop and think. Such statistics are impossible to gather, but it is a good bet that if they could be, we would discover that managers are more likely to change their own thinking than to take on the whole world, especially when the odds against them are so high.

If the manager has good working relations with those above him in the hierarchy, another alternative is to try to negotiate some changes in the demands of the company so that the manager will not have to bend so many of his own convictions or scrap them. When this talk is instituted, it may become clear that upper echelons were simply not thinking of the possible consequences to the managers at lower levels, and they may quite easily and quickly change their demands to something more reasonable. Naturally, negotiations of this sort are extremely delicate, both to initiate and to carry on, for the manager is actually questioning the thinking (perhaps even the ethics) of those above him in the organization. This can never be done thoughtlessly or with a heavy hand. Much planning and careful evaluation must go into this situation.

Another alternative followed by many managers is to stall for time while trying to resolve the dilemma. The manager is ordinarily acute enough to find a million excuses for the delay of a given project. This method is tough, for it will throw an almost intolerable extra burden on the manager. He is going to have to be doubly busy, first, in finding adroit methods of performing his stall and, second, in rather frantically looking for some way to solve his problem.

The pressure is not reduced by the fact that the manager will be operating in complete secrecy. He dare not take *anyone* into his confidence while performing this maneuver. It is also evident that he is playing Russian roulette, for if he is discovered there can be only one result. Nevertheless, for many managers this is more palatable than some of the methods previously considered, since it does not entail an immediate sacrifice of principles and modus operandi. For a time, in any case, the manager will be allowed to retain his self-respect and at least the illusion of being self-determinant in his operations.

There is another obvious alternative, and this one is the scariest and toughest of them all: The manager may simply refuse to bend. What if he stands by his own principles and will not alter them for company expediency? What chance does he have for survival if he goes this way? There are no set answers to these onerous questions, and every situation will have to be played as unique. In the first place, there is no way a manager can pursue this course without quite openly challenging the hierarchy. There are only two likely responses to this sort of challenge by those above him. The first and more predictable one is that the manager will be considered expendable and will lose his job. The second one is that, because of his previous valuable service, he will be allowed one "deviation" from company policy but will be put on notice that this kind of behavior will not be tolerated again.

A third, but rather remote, possibility is that the manager's actions will arouse the admiration and respect of those above him and that company policy will be changed to conform to his beliefs and tenets. This has happened—a few times. Serendipity can be the only result for the manager who follows this course. He has the knowledge that he remains his own man and that in the final analysis he is *not* simply a creature of his employers. Even if he loses and is forced to terminate, he still has this feeling, and for many people this is enough to make the entire battle worthwhile.

The whole matter of the manager's personal integrity receives far too little attention from the public and from management itself. It is either tacitly assumed, by most people, or openly scorned and scoffed at—by a Machiavellian group of managers whose sole measure of success is in terms of personal aggrandizement. This attitude cannot be deplored deeply enough, because it is a terribly insidious kind of poison.

Managers, for their very position, command respect from a certain segment of the public. They are opinion makers as well as change agents. If they actually believe in personal aggrandizement and are not hesitant about communicating their views to friends, subordinates, and customers, this philosophy can be spread over a large area with completely subversive results. The day the American manager really loses his integrity and refuses to stand by personal principle, we are a lost nation. Political decay can be overcome quickly by an aroused public; if our managerial population is suffering from dry rot, we are in serious trouble.

CAN YOU REALLY WIN THE BATTLE?

The answer to whether managers can really win a battle with their employers has to be a qualified "maybe." Many variables are involved in any situation leading to a conflict of interest, but naturally the two greatest are you, the manager, and the company you represent. Taking first your situation, we can only reinforce the fact that if this conflict leads to a real test of your basic principles, you are bound to be a loser one way or the other. Either you will compromise your beliefs, and thereby feel degraded, or you will be in an untenable position with your company management and will probably find it necessary to terminate—that is, unless company representatives above you find it possible to alter their position. Such a confrontation between you and your employers will at least tell you one thing: the value they put on your services.

At this point we might do well to indicate a major change occurring today in the attitudes of younger employees toward their working life. It is apparent that the Protestant ethic is no longer the accepted way of life, bought and paid for by every young American man or woman. Many of them are telling us in no uncertain terms that they have values much higher than the purely material rewards for working and that they intend to pursue these other goals quite actively. If they do not find these within their working scene, so much the worse for the job—it will sink to second-rate importance in their thinking. In other words, many young people are *coming* to the job with a built-in conflict of interest. To the traditional manager, this situation is either puzzling or frightening—perhaps both. It is nearly impossible for him to empathize with young people who talk this way, mainly because the older manager doesn't really believe that they are sincere. He is nagged by the recurring thought that he is the victim of a gigantic "put on," and this angers him.

The traditionalist must alter his approach to these young men and women, because there is no real evidence of insincerity on their part. It is true that if he has a little patience and waits for them to become entrapped in their own materialistic responsibilities, they will probably change their orientation. But at this particular time they really do have values of higher priority than the money ones.

It would be fallacious and simplistic to assume that it is only the young whose thinking has been changed in these areas. There have been many cases where the thinking of the offspring has influenced that of the parent. Many parents see a real logic in what their children are telling them and are beginning to reexamine their own objectives and value sets. It is no longer headline news to hear of an eminently successful business person who suddenly leaves his or her career at its zenith to strike off in a new and completely strange direction, with significantly less monetary returns from the new job. We are hearing these people talk about "self-fulfillment," and "higher purposes in living," and they are saying it with a quiet dignity which makes a questioning of their sincerity nearly impossible.

This indicates that we can expect conflicts of interest to increase in both number and severity within the next few years. It also means that *management in general is going to have to make some basic changes in its thinking,* or it will wake up some morning to find itself an anachronism, totally out of touch with the reality of modern living. Who is to say that the philosophy and main objectives of an organization cannot change just as much as those of its individual members? The one characteristic more than any other which propelled America into world preeminence in the fields of business and industry was our ability to remain flexible, to accept change and build it into our daily lives. If we lose that ability we are dead in the water.

Perhaps the thing that managers have to be aware of most of all is any sign of the start of a conflict-of-interest situation, so that they can resolve it before it reaches the panic-crisis stage. It is always easier to dampen down a small campfire than to fight a raging forest fire.

Once more, we can only say that, given a modicum of patience and good sense on the part of both the manager involved and his principals, it will usually be possible to reduce conflicts of interest without any serious casualties on either side.

11

THE MANAGERIAL
MENTALITY

There can hardly be any question that managers think differently in many areas than do the people who work with and for them. This is both necessary and right; the manager's function is different from that of the people who actually make the products or perform the services, and his approach to this job has to be from a different frame of reference.

IMPORTANCE OF A MANAGERIAL MENTAL SET

If the manager were to look at problems on the job in exactly the same way as the people who work for him, the job would never be managed. In the first place, the worker is naturally inclined to see his problems from a selfish angle, while the supervisor must keep an objective frame of mind and in many cases sacrifice his own wishes for the good of the organization. This we can expect from only a minuscule proportion of the hourly paid or nonexempt employees.

At the same time he is discharging this managerial duty, the supervisor must be prepared to sell to his employees the necessity for a certain decision which may be contrary to what they want. Neither can he expect his people to accept very often the argument of "what is good for the company." The persuasion is going to have to be couched in other terms if there is to be any chance of its acceptance by employees. Many times it *is* possible to point out advantages to them not immediately apparent when a decision has been announced.

It is the job of the manager to be alert to these hidden factors and to be ready to use them in soothing his subordinates.

The manager's superiors are also concerned about the depth and breadth of his conceptualization of the company's activities. As he rises in the hierarchy, the manager's conceptual skills must continue to increase. This facet of his thinking is an absolute must for his planning activities. The way his managerial decisions and actions mesh with others' is as important as any other part of his job. It is a truism that today's manager will not be able to plan for himself or his crew alone. Too many others are directly or indirectly involved in and affected by what he does. One more time, we can only point out that modern management is a team effort, and its success will be conditioned by the thinking and actions of *every* manager in an enterprise.

Another reason for a manager's thinking differently is purely self-protective. As already indicated, he will not be successful as a manager unless he alters his mental processes upon promotion. This matter of protection, obviously enough, extends beyond the manager himself. He will also have to protect his people from situations inimical to them. What is likely to hurt them is also likely to hurt the manager, and the leader must be prepared to take protective action for all involved. He cannot expect his subordinates to be aware enough of certain situations to take action for themselves; this must be initiated by the group leader.

All of the preceding leads to consideration of another fundamental truth: The manager is placed in a position of responsibility and leadership. There are many aspects of leadership which are uncertain and unclear to observers, but one sure and certain thing is that the leader must think differently from his followers. He must of necessity *go before* the other members of the group. The leader stands out in front, and his thinking must be in advance as well. So it becomes a matter of both *quality and timing* when we speak of the mental set of leaders.

This is not to say that the leader will always be in movement. There are many times when he will have to make a considered judgment before taking action, and he must be prepared to withstand considerable pressure from others while he is thinking the situation through. This is one of the more traumatic situations of leadership; many times it subjects the leader to criticism both unfair and unfounded from those not aware of the complexity of the situation. Here again we are looking at a different kind of mental set from that of the worker in the ranks. The latter would be more than likely to submit to peer-group pressures and go along with them without fully considering all implications of the action.

Finally, and certainly not of least importance, the manager must think differently upon promotion in order to realize the fullest measure of job satisfaction. The managers who are most comfortable and successful in their jobs are those who self-actualize at work. They get a private joy from seeing themselves growing as they satisfy metaneeds many others don't have. The fact that the manager must think differently and ahead of his people is at the same time an onerous task and one of the major rewards of this leadership position. It is sometimes tough because it makes managers vulnerable, but at all times gratifying as they accept the challenge and beat it. Incidentally, the deepest, toughest, and most ongoing competition the manager meets is not with his peers but within himself. Every time a gain is made, the goals must be raised, so that the next adventure will still be a challenge and a thrill.

HOW DOES A MANAGER THINK DIFFERENTLY?

One noticeable difference in the way a manager thinks is that his frame of reference is much broader. Until one becomes a manager, it is quite natural to think in a fairly selfish framework. "What's in it for me?" is the first question usually arising in the job situation whenever a new thing is contemplated. The manager, however, is not allowed this luxury. He has to do his thinking in terms of the entire organization, its objectives, and all ramifications likely to arise.

At the same time, it is understood that the manager must think in terms of *both* people and things. Before, he could confine his job thinking for the most part to people—himself, his peers, and the boss. Once the change is made in job status to supervision and management, it becomes mandatory for the manager to think a great deal about things. Capital investments, materials, equipment, and products weigh heavily on his mind at all times. True, before his promotion, the worker naturally does a little thinking about the product he is working on, but in no way does this thinking approximate in either amount or depth what the manager has to do in getting his job done.

Sometimes, in fact, the manager can hardly be blamed for assuming that there is a deliberate perversity of the inanimate. Moreover, it will probably come to him as a shock to learn that things and people must be integrated on the job; it is no longer possible to think about the one without also considering the other. Interactions between things and people can be highly unpredictable, and many times the results are far from salutary. It is this the manager must be prepared for on the job.

Now also, for the first time in his or her life perhaps, the manager discovers the absolute necessity of thinking as objectively as it is possible for a human being to do. We are all aware that it is impossible to be totally objective about anything, but the manager must undertake a severe personal discipline to be sure that personal biases do not cloud his mental processes. It should be remembered that there is a wide range of differences in the innate ability of people to think objectively. To some, it is nearly impossible; to others, it comes quite naturally.

In any event, this trait is one of the essentials for continuing success in management, and if the newly appointed manager has had difficulty with it, his superiors should make an immediate effort to upgrade his ability to think in objective terms. Like so many other things in our lives, a habit must be formed in this direction, and it is a sad commentary on life that the "good" habits we find necessary are always the most difficult to acquire. Constant attention to practice is the answer.

Another difference in managerial thinking is that attitudes

toward peers and upper management will naturally vary from those toward subordinates. This dichotomy in the thinking of a manager also comes hard at first. It seems vaguely dishonest to the new manager to think differently about people in different job situations. Actually, this differentiation is as natural as the coming and going of the days. The manager has only to remind himself how his own thinking has been changed to see that his subordinates (former peers) are now different from him. They have had no occasion to change their thinking, while he has had.

The acquisition of this new and different approach is one of the hurdles the manager must handle immediately, and it is the source of a major number of failures on the part of newly promoted managers. The manager will find it necessary and useful to go through a more or less formal analysis of these differences and to place values on their importance to his future success. This type of mental reinforcement ordinarily will make it much easier for the manager to reorganize both his thinking and his actions toward the people with whom he is associated on the job.

A final way in which the manager's thinking is different is that he must do a lot more of it now than formerly. When he was "on the line," in most cases the job could be mastered within a relatively short time and little active thought was required to keep it rolling satisfactorily. Not so now. The manager will almost never get to the point where more thinking is not required on the job. Conditions, things, and people are all changing too rapidly for him ever to stop making ongoing assessments of his position. What was workable and useful yesterday on the job may not be so today, and almost certainly will not be tomorrow.

This matter of unflagging mental alertness should be obvious to any observer of the job scene, but it is amazing how many people fail to recognize this factor. They make a totally false assumption that promotion into management is a difference in degree but not in kind. On the contrary, the day employees accept a promotion into management, they will undergo a greater change in their lives than will ever occur again. Their entire mental and emotional nature must of necessity be altered to enter that strange land, and they will never be the same again.

HOW DO YOU ACQUIRE THIS MENTAL SET?

We have repeatedly reinforced the idea that the manager must think differently from other working people. Let us now examine the methodology by which managers can get this new and unusual mental set. First of all, there must be a recognition and identification of the differences by the manager himself. His first job is to recognize both that there is a managerial mentality and that it is a necessary part of the manager's armamentarium on the job. It is essential to master these preliminaries *before* promotion into management, because no person can be effective in a managerial job until these things have been accomplished.

The selection and promotion of management people is now recognized as one of the most important jobs of a company's management group. Most companies of any size are coming to formalize these procedures, so that some sort of controls can be evolved and applied to the process. However, in all too many cases this aspect of the selection and preliminary preparation of candidates is overlooked, or at least poorly done. Managers who have spent some time in their jobs successfully seem to forget how great a change took place in their thinking during the transition into the job, and they may actually be confused if someone points out to them the necessity for this kind of mental readjustment on the part of candidates for promotion.

However, there can be no doubt that it is the responsibility of the sponsoring manager to see that his candidate has been thoroughly briefed on how he will have to change his thinking. In addition, sufficient time should be allowed before promotion for the prospective manager to become accustomed to this new way of mental life. All people involved should be aware that we can never forecast with any degree of certainty how long this process will be for a given individual. Some will seem to pick it up intuitively, while others will require many months to reorient themselves.

One of the best ways to teach this process is to make use of cases. The sponsoring manager can derive case studies from events going on in the company, many times as they are actually developing. These will, of course, have the direct and urgent appeal of an ongoing story for the manager in training. His prophecies of what will happen a little later in such a situation can be a vehicle for a wealth of fine counseling by the sponsoring manager. In addition, there are hundreds of prepared cases in textbooks, many of which have become classics over the years. If this method is used, the sponsor can chart the development of managerial thinking in the candidate just as a doctor charts his patient's progress. True quantification will not be possible, but the sponsor most certainly will be able to get a good idea of what is going on in the candidate's mind.

Naturally enough, the prospect should also be active in his own behalf. A manager should not have to be spoonfed, and it is the candidate's responsibility to do some thinking for himself and then to check with his mentor for criticism and comment. The acid test of real progress on the part of the prospect is when he generates his own cases from his observations of what is going on about him and brings them to his coach, rather than waiting for the latter to hand some to him.

At the same time, the candidate should be doing a heavy amount of reading, Most certainly, his sponsor should ensure that he is completely familiar with classic management writing. The works of Taylor, Drucker, Likert, Odiorne, McGregor, Maslow, Herzberg, Glasser, and Argyris should be mandatory, but certainly his reading should not be restricted to this corps of stalwarts. Care should be taken to pick a representative group of periodicals for the candidate to read on a continuing basis.

We have come close to full circle now in the matter of the prospect's need for a solid, though still developing, philosophy of management. A real and lasting decision must be made about the general direction in which the manager proposes to go and about the particular methodology by which he intends to achieve his goals. As already stated, we are long past the time when managers could fly by the seat of their pants. It is obvious that when the prospective manager does solidify the concept of his own managerial philosophy he will be far downstream toward achieving the mental set we have been talking about.

It is appropriate here to recapitulate some of the things necessary in the selection and preparation of a management candidate. First, and fundamental to everything else, it must be determined to everyone's satisfaction that the candidate has made the "management decision." Does he *really* want to be a manager, or does the job just seem glamorous to him? Or has he been misinformed about the size of a beginning manager's salary? If the answer to the question about the management decision is affirmative, the next step is to set about helping the candidate acquire the managerial mental set by the methodologies discussed in this chapter.

One thing is for sure: There is no handy, simplified formula which will ensure the making of a manager. It is a long, complicated, and arduous process, and perhaps this is just as well, since the process itself can serve as a screening operation par excellence.

WHAT ARE THE GAINS AND FOR WHOM?

By the time we have thought through the elements of this chapter, the answer to the question of who gains from the proper training of managers has begun to emerge. Everyone concerned benefits from the fact that the manager has discovered and adopted the new way of thinking essential to his job. His managers above him in the line will recognize his bettered performance; his peers will gain respect for him as a professional; his subordinates will begin to see that his leadership has scope and depth. It is essential to recognize how much the mental set of a manager has to do with the quality and effectiveness of his leadership. It is impossible for a manager to lead intuitively — there are too many traps along the road to evade with anything but the clearest and most hard-headed thinking.

As indicated, gains from this activity of managers will appear in every part of the organization, at every level, and in all aspects of the enterprise. One of the most noticeable will be an increased self-confidence and increased confidence in the entire organization by all its members. If they are assured that their managers are constantly thinking in the particular way they must to do their jobs properly, any errors which will naturally occur will be more easily forgiven and forgotten.

A second major gain will be in shortened times required for decisions. Employees quite naturally base a large part of their judgment of managers on the number of correct decisions made by their leaders, and they are much more inclined to be comfortable under managers who are correct most of the time. Of course, it is much easier to make judgments of first- and second-line managers than of those higher in the organization, because the decisions made by middle and upper management are not implemented for months and sometimes for years. Thus top management, dealing as it does with decisions which will be carried out two, three, five, or ten years from now, cannot be judged with any immediacy by the rest of the employees of the firm.

A third gain from this activity will be in better interpersonal relationships throughout the organization. When managers are thinking properly in a managerial frame of reference, their own tensions and doubts will be reduced to the point where they can interact more smoothly with their peers and subordinates. The latter will also be affected for the better as they see managers calm and composed in their dealings with others in the organization. The uncertainties which arise from fuzzy thinking are great breeders of strife and dissension among the members of any group.

A fourth major gain from having managers think as managers is actually a threefold benefit: a better chance for survival of the enterprise, a better profit picture, and a better chance for continued growth of the business. In other words, it is insurance for the firm and job insurance for the managers within it. It would be fallacious to assert that this is the only condition for these happenings, but it certainly is one of the major causative factors, and they could hardly occur without proper managerial thinking.

A final and not inconsiderable gain is the heightened reputation of the enterprise among customers and outsiders. It is never possible to hide the presence or absence of proper managerial thinking from objective observers not associated with the organization. They can spot both causes and results of managerial action within any firm; from those, it is relatively easy to analyze which is cause and which is effect. Once again, it is highly reinforcing to a manager's thinking and to his general mental health to know he or she is working for a concern which is well thought of by the general public.

It is a priceless asset for a manager to be able to take real and deep pride from the fact that he is working for a given company. It is also possible for a manager to believe that his company's poor reputation is undeserved, but its presence will still have a negative effect on his thinking and leave him uneasy. This is not conducive to effective work over a long period of time. When our own good opinion of our employers is reinforced by the general reputation among outsiders, we have an ideal climate in which to work productively.

To recapitulate, there is a logical chain of development in the matter of proper managerial thinking. The manager must first make the discovery that his thinking will of necessity change in both kind and amount as he accepts managerial responsibility. Once this has been accomplished, he must find the way in which it is most comfortable for him to learn to think as a manager. Lastly, he must practice this new way of thinking assiduously until he has firmly established it as a habit, so that he performs it unconsciously and never deviates from it while on the job.

Once this happens, the manager can begin to enjoy the benefits which will accrue both to him and to his company, safe in the knowledge that this new way of mental life is the best insurance he will have for effective performance in the managerial world. By this time, he will also have become convinced that the world of management is indeed a separate place, like none other, with some very rigid requirements for different kinds of behavior and thinking than are operative in the other facets of his life. Managers constitute a small minority of the working population, and they are noticeable for their differences from other employees.

12

SO NOW WHERE?

It is time that we stop, recapitulate, and put a capstone on our process of evolving a managerial philosophy. We have looked at the essential elements which must be considered and now we should put them in perspective. Even more important, we should consider what is ahead of us as managers in the foreseeable future. There are some new variables which impinge on the management scene and they must be considered fully, both for their initial impact and for what they may do later.

THE RESPONSIBILITY FOR MANAGERIAL LEADERSHIP

Managers have always had a basic responsibility for the leadership of their people, for leadership interactions with their peers, and for a readiness to accept leadership in other segments of their lives. This comes as a natural fallout of the fact that they have chosen to enter a small minority of the work force whose job by definition has facets of leadership in it. It would seem that this older and more traditional part of the manager's job would be universally recognized and accepted by anyone entering a managerial position, but such is not always the case. Many, many failures occur each year because newly promoted managers simply do not accept leadership responsibility in their jobs. Such a situation is invariably fatal to the career of the man or woman who fails in this area.

Higher members of management, in making recommendations for promoting people into their first management position, seem to assume that this facet of the job will be completely understood by the candidates, but that just does not always happen. A person who is ambitious for upward mobility can be dazzled by the glamor of the position, and it is easy to over-look this crucially important aspect of the job. Naturally enough, this failure occurs when the manager does not make the necessary decisions involved in his leadership duties and thereby abdicates a large part of his responsibility, in many cases without even realizing where he is failing.

It should be apparent that the real problem in these cases lies with ranks of higher managers who fail to probe for this awareness before making their promotions and who fail to do the necessary training before putting the candidates into managerial positions. There are two things which might happen if these steps were recognized as necessary by upper management. First, if the full spectrum of managerial duties, including leadership duties, were made completely clear to the candidates, they might be turned off and lose their desire for advancement. Second, if after having this part of the job fully clarified to them they still are eager to go, a little training from their seniors might avert disaster on the job. Most real candidates for management will recognize this as a natural part of the job when it is pointed out to them, and they can then prepare themselves properly.

As previously indicated, there is a new and unique variable entering the scene in the life of the American manager. For one of the very few times in the history of our country our political leaders are either abdicating or subverting their responsibilities. Everywhere we turn, we find people in high office either admitting venality or at least being charged with crimes and misdemeanors. There is one inevitable corollary to this situation: Someone, or some group, must pick up the reins of leadership if our country is to survive, let alone maintain its traditional position of leadership in the world. There is no more logical set of candidates for this new role than the business and industrial leadership of our country.

Actually, in our recently burgeoning international business activities we have already entered into this in a minor but growing effort. In our interactions with businessmen of other countries we have learned that we cannot wait for our government to give us the necessary signals by which to operate. So long as the American manager is careful to stay within the guidelines established by the American government and the other governments with which he is dealing, he is free to negotiate as he chooses with foreign clients. With one or two recent exceptions, such as the Russian wheat purchase of 1972, the Yankee trader has never had too much difficulty in at least maintaining a competitive position with his clients and customers anywhere in the world. We can only assume that this characteristic is still extant among our managers and that they will continue to hold their own in international commerce.

But it is not in international business that the American manager can do the best service to his country; currently, it is within his own domestic scene. The American citizenry will find it immensely comforting to be able to look to the management population for the leadership now lacking on the political scene; in all actuality, there is nowhere else that they can look for the stabilizing influences inherent in good leadership. Although this presents a new challenge to the manager and will most certainly add to his overall burden, it should not be an insurmountable task. In the long run it can only add to his stature and rate of growth, and the final advantages will accrue to the manager just as much as to the people who are depending on managers everywhere for this added effort. In any event, the challenge is there, and it is up to the managers of our country to pick up the dare and to make the most of a new opportunity.

MAPPING THE UNCHARTED WAYS

One of the more easily understood elements of the manager's job to the lay public is that, in its position of leadership, it entails a frequent probing of different and unknown methods of getting the job done. The changes which hit us so often and with such devastating impact mean that the manager must constantly be on the lookout for new ways of solving the problems which inevitably arise.

For the comfort of the bewildered or fearful manager, there is a methodology of attacking new problems, and it has a better than even chance for success whenever it is applied on the job. If the problem facing the manager appears to be unfamiliar, the best first step is to make a quick run-through of methods already at hand for problem solving. Perhaps one of them will work in this situation and there will be no need for innovation or the design of an exotic new approach. These are the easy cases, but we cannot expect this to be true for every problem faced by today's boss.

If none of the traditional problem-solving methods seems applicable to the situation, the manager must rely on his own inventiveness, persistence, and perception. By all odds the best method here is to enlist the help of other members of the work group at once. The sooner they become involved, the better the chance the manager has for getting and making use of their best mental efforts. There are some problems which do not lend themselves to group effort in their solution, but for the most part the kinds of problems the manager meets from day to day can be solved more easily by recruiting the efforts of many people. The manager's job here is to act as judge and referee; he *is* the boss, and it is his duty to make the decision of "go" or "no go" for any particular item.

Once the thinking of the work group has been pooled, it is quite likely that possible alternatives will start to be identified. Some of these will have much more face validity than others. Once again, the manager must make the choice of which one to use first, which to revert to if the first one fails, and so on.

It is highly probable, in the complexity of the business and industrial world of today, that even this group effort may not produce an alternative which looks too inviting to the manager. This is his cue to call in the help of the experts: the representatives of some of the staff departments found in all modern businesses. The judicious use of staff people by line managers is what distinguishes the men from the boys. A word of caution: The manager cannot afford to just dump his problem on staff people and expect them to come up with a foolproof solution. The key is, of course, to work *with* staff members in the hope that their specialized expertise will provide insights leading to a successful solution by the manager himself.

If the solution developed by the manager is a new one—or apparently so—it is his manifest duty to communicate this novel method as quickly as possible to everyone who might have an interest in it. It is difficult enough to stay afloat without hiding something which might be of use to other managers. The manager might have an immediate instinct to keep hidden from his competition this methodology which has proved useful to him. He will, for a time at least, have an advantage over those who are unaware of what he has done. We should consider whether this is an acceptable managerial attitude. Can we afford to have managers acting for selfish reasons, either for themselves individually or for the sole benefit of their company? It would appear that we cannot.

Our nation's economic well-being is no longer the sum of the good for a group of individual companies. We must turn our efforts and our attention to the fullest sort of cooperation on a national basis if our country is to survive as one of the world's leaders. This concept includes interdisciplinary cooperation as well as that within a single industry or family of industries. So, on the basis of the manager's acceptance of this philosophy, it becomes abundantly clear that when a new solution has been found and it is certain that it is workable, there must be no delay in proper communication of the findings to others interested.

The final step in problem solving is to ensure that an objective and thorough postevaluation is done of the entire procedure. It sometimes happens that a solution which appears perfect at first glance later turns sour and proves not to be the answer at all. The manager has the obligation not to lose track of what has happened for a reasonable time after the conclusion of the effort. There must be consistent monitoring of the immediate and long-range results of what has been done before final judgment can be rendered on the entire process.

This new managerial duty of innovative problem solving is fast coming to be one of the major criteria by which a business or industrial leader's work is measured. After all, if every problem managers faced required only established methods and solutions, our constant worry about the quality of our managers would be reduced almost to the vanishing point. Because this is not the case, managers must be constantly alert to each and every problem facing them and must decide as early as possible whether a given problem is new and different enough to require an innovative solution. These decisions, plus what the manager does in the process of innovation, will tell us the quality of his managerial activities.

GETTING FEEDBACK

Nowhere in the field of management is it so important to get good feedback as in the area of progress and innovation. The communicative process in other areas of the managerial job can be controlled fairly easily; this is not so in this part of the job. The manager concerned with instituting a new process or an innovation will have to do several things in order to ensure getting the necessary feedback.

First, it is totally the manager's responsibility to supply complete information about his project to everyone who will have any connection with it. This is easier to say than it is to do, because in many cases it is not entirely clear just who *will* be involved before the project's pilot run has been completed. The ripples from casting the pebbles into the pond are not predictable the first time around. Suffice it to say that the manager responsible would do far better to overcommunicate than to leave out someone who will later prove indispensable to the whole cycle.

Second, the manager in charge will have to make many value judgments of the feedback he does receive. Since the project is new (and probably exciting), he will ordinarily not have much difficulty enlisting his respondents around the circle, but it is quite likely that he will have less than an easy time evaluating the things they do communicate to him. This is due to the fact that he has no data bank of previous experience with which to compare what he hears and learns from respondents.

Fairly quickly, of course, the manager will get either similar or conflicting reports from the various people he has keyed into the operation, and from these there will eventually appear some guidelines for judging the feedback. But at first he must of necessity feel his way almost blindly, and his only recourse is his personal gut judgment of the validity of the things he is hearing. Naturally, since he is the creator of the innovation that is being flown for the first or second time, he will have to make as careful a judgment as possible until factual data can be supplied.

Third, the frequency of feedback must be significantly higher at first than will be necessary when the innovation starts to become established. The manager in charge will have to make a real pest of himself during the shakedown cruise in order to get enough facts to make the necessary final judgments. If the project is thought to be really critical to the ongoing success of the organization, it is probable that these inputs will be required on a daily basis during the initial go-round. This may be a nuisance for some of the respondents, but it clearly is not an unreasonable request, because of the critical nature of the feedback to the success of the venture. The project manager may have to make some drastic changes in his procedures as a result of these first bits of feedback, and most of his peers will be reasonable enough to recognize this fact.

Finally, and by no means least important, the innovator should be conscious of the necessity for getting expert advice from others not connected with his activity. Granted, as we have seen, that the inventor of the new process should have a better feeling for what is going on than anyone else. Nonetheless, his ego involvement will be so great that he would do well to call for the objective judgments of others before making the final "go" or "no go" decision for the new project.

One way of accomplishing these matters is for the manager to simply describe to his "referee" what has been happening and relay the feedback which has been received so far. The impartial observer may get enough from this procedure to make a meaningful response. If he does not and is willing to do so, he should become personally involved in the project, acquaint himself thoroughly with it, and then follow it for a cycle or two to get better understanding of what he is seeing. Obviously, this may be quite time-consuming in the case of an involved or complex operation, but most managers are interested in innovations, especially when they are occurring in their own enterprises. Again, they are professional enough to sense an ongoing duty to offer this kind of aid and assistance.

As can be seen, this process is simply an extension—or an intensification—of the communicative duties every manager has constantly with him. As has been observed many times, it is the failure to obtain feedback—or close the loop—which is the most common cause of communications breakdowns in the business world. Often we make incorrect assumptions about the receipt and understanding of what we have transmitted. The subject under discussion is so crystal-clear in our own minds that it is inconceivable to us that anyone else could fail to understand it thoroughly. The fact remains that for many reasons this is not always so. Each of us carries innumerable baffles which can distort the incoming message; unless the sender is constantly aware of this, the result is only too frequently a breakdown in the entire communicative process. The innovative manager in particular is the one who should never lose sight of this fundamental fact of life.

MANAGEMENT AND THE FUTURE

Practically all that has been said in this short book has been put into a frame of reference of the present. We have examined what today's manager has to do to be competitive and the conceptual image he must derive of management as a profession and a way of life. But the real test of managerial leadership lies not in today's activities but in what managers will do next year, next decade, and next century. It is important to reinforce the point that managers must rapidly increase the measure of their leadership, not only in their own group and the enterprise for which they work, but in the community, the state, and the nation. We can have no way of knowing how long we shall be faced with a dearth of strong, charismatic political leadership, but so long as we are, someone must step in to fill the void, and managers are the logical group to take over this function.

Facing this hugely increased leadership responsibility will require of every manager a personal philosophy that serves as a guide for his actions and as a navigational instrument for his career voyage. Choices will continue to become more difficult, because of the complex matrix into which our business and industrial organizations are placed. Major business decisions are no longer a matter of a simple choice between black and white; a veritable rainbow of alternatives presents itself to the responsible manager in every major decision he is required to make. He must put these alternatives one by one up against the benchmarks of his managerial philosophy before making his choice, and once made he must have the courage to go ahead, even if the prospect is murky and unclear from where he is standing.

The quality of courage has never been so important in the managerial makeup as it is today. It takes a strong person to put a career on the line every time a major decision must be made, and that is exactly what is happening to management people. This trend will become stronger in the future, because things will get more complex rather than simpler.

The day of the professional manager is already here; the profession of management is still a few years away from us, principally because there is no clear-cut and definitive managerial philosophy which has wide acceptance throughout the managerial ranks. The body of special knowledge we are rapidly acquiring; the conceptualization of the entire field still eludes us for the most part. Of course, here and there we see some great business leaders who have a well-developed and open managerial philosophy of their own, but they have been less than eloquent in communicating it to their peers and their juniors. This one last commitment they must accept, onerous though it may be for them. All people who work have a right to be guided by managers who know exactly how they want to operate—anything less than that is too dangerous for their group and their enterprises.

One last observation is in line here: It is long overdue that the business community devise and implement a "professional" managerial designation similar to that of the Certified Public Accountant. The MBAs so eagerly sought by young managers today are a step in the right direction, but they don't fill all the requirements. Their content and makeup are so widely variable that the simple designation of MBA after a person's name tells us less than nothing about his or her professional preparation for the management field. The accountants have their professional designation; the engineers have theirs. Why shouldn't managers get the same privilege of pursuing a good, tough course of study which can end in the possibility for true professionalism in their performance? Managers—and the people who work for them—have this coming to them.